MW00460773

Praise for *Finding Fortunato*

"I love chocolate stories almost as much as I love chocolate makers, and this is a good one. It's the swashbuckling, cinematic version of what it takes to be an international entrepreneur. It's not just about the chocolate; it's about a journey we can all choose to go on."

—Seth Godin, *New York Times* Bestselling Author,
Linchpin and *The Song of Significance*

"A wonderful international business adventure about chasing dreams, never giving up, and the power of win/win relationships."

—Jon Gordon, Bestselling Author, *The Power of Positive Leadership*

"This is the Indiana Jones of chocolate stories! Dan and Brian's heartwarming story and the entrepreneurial lessons of tenacity and value creation make for an incredible combination—like cacao and sugar. Adam does a fantastic job of keeping the book tight. This is a feel-good story meant for the modern day."

—Craig Ballantyne, Author, *The Perfect Day Formula*

"Throughout history, humans have sought the origins of beginnings. The discovery of the rarest cacao at the headwaters of the Amazon River is a journey of such exploration. *Finding Fortunato*, from cacao tree to chocolate, will take you on an adventure."

—Paul Edward & Crystal Mier, International Chocolatiers;
Founders, Chef Rubber; Philanthropists; and Explorers

"Being part of the greatest cacao discovery of our generation bears responsibility for the owners of the land in the 'Jurassic Park of cacao' and the unique genetic material. Crafting the best chocolate from it is a sensual gift to the world. I am proud to be part of this amazing story."

—Franz Ziegler, Award-Winning Author and World-Renowned Pastry Chef

"It is rare to read a story that truly transports you to a world of indulgence, intrigue, and adventure. So beautifully written . . . as if I walked every step of the jungle and tasted each bite along with the author. I wanted more."

—Janice Feldman, Founder, JANUS et Cie, and Winner,
ICON of Industry Award for Hospitality

FINDING FORTUNATO

FINDING FORTUNATO

How a Peruvian Adventure Inspired the Sweet Success of a Family Chocolate Business

ADAM PEARSON

Matt Holt Books
An Imprint of BenBella Books, Inc.
Dallas, TX

Matt Holt is an imprint of BenBella Books, Inc.
10440 N. Central Expressway
Suite 800
Dallas, TX 75231
benbellabooks.com
Send feedback to feedback@benbellabooks.com.

BenBella and *Matt Holt* are federally registered trademarks.

Printed in the United States of America
10 9 8 7 6 5 4 3 2 1

Library of Congress Control Number: 2023049259
ISBN 9781637744925 (hardcover)
ISBN 9781637744932 (electronic)

Editing by Katie Dickman
Copyediting by Ginny Glass
Proofreading by Denise Pangia and Cape Cod Compositors, Inc.
Text design and composition by PerfecType, Nashville, TN
Cover design by Brigid Pearson
Cover image © Shutterstock / Belchatina (cacao); Shutterstock / Istry Istry (candy bar)
Printed by Lake Book Manufacturing

Dedicated to my dad and brother, my heroes.

CONTENTS

CHAPTER 1

ME

You don't get to choose your family. Mine are entrepreneurs. It's a unique kind of fate. Your parents, loving though they may be, are around less, and you're left to figure out life on your own more than other kids. You see daring attempts at audacious goals and have a front-row seat to the crushing defeats that often come with bold risk-taking.

My dad, Dan Pearson, is a serial entrepreneur who has suffered more than his fair share of defeats. Now age eighty-three, he is a world-class authority on bouncing back.

The extraordinary thing about my dad is that he was right so often, but the cash results didn't reflect it. In the 1970s, he started one of the world's first cattle investment funds. He and his partners were making money hand over fist until the fateful day President Richard Nixon, responding to hyperinflation, instituted severe price controls on beef. The fund was wiped out.

In the 1980s, he reconstructed the historic Horton Grand Hotel in downtown San Diego's Gaslamp Quarter district. He helped my mom build a theater next door in another historic building. Both buildings still stand as monuments to his rightness. The property is worth millions today. Our family should still own it, but alas, my dad lost it through a combination of bad luck and misplaced trust in a dishonest investor.

Losing the hotel was a crushing blow for our family. Until then, my free time as a child was largely spent roaming the hotel. When I was hungry, I went to the kitchen and got a fresh blueberry muffin from the chef. When I was bored, I went outside to play with my brother, Brian, and his friends, who worked as valets. For dinner, I sat in the bar and ate happy hour food. My parents usually worked late.

At school, I was smart but disruptive. The constant refrain at the dreaded parent-teacher conferences was "Adam is so capable, if he would just apply himself!" It was hard to get fired up about worksheets and deskwork after roaming your dad's hotel and eating happy hour food for dinner. Walking the floors of our hotel, talking to the staff, learning how things worked—that was my sweet spot. I believed I was going to take over the place someday. I needed to be ready. Too bad it wasn't in the cards.

When I was eleven, we lost the hotel. Its construction had been timed to coincide with the opening of a new convention center in downtown. Unfortunately, the convention center got delayed by several years.

Dad tirelessly fought the good fight. He raised extra equity and lined up additional credit, which he personally guaranteed. He promoted day and night to attract guests. He did everything possible to keep the hotel alive. Through sheer grit and hustle, Dad survived until the convention center was on the verge of completion. A little longer and we would have made it. But ultimately, Dad had no choice but to declare personal bankruptcy and walk away.

I recall a particular time standing with my dad in front of the hotel shortly before we lost it. We looked up at this beautiful creation that he had built brick by brick, and he was overwhelmed with satisfaction that his share in the hotel was worth about $10 million, and someday he would leave it to me and Brian. Two years later, at age fifty-five, my dad was washed out and nearly broke. He had worked on that project for fourteen years.

Five months before losing the hotel, tragedy struck one of our family's best friends. Azim Khamisa was an investment banker my dad met while working on financing for the hotel. Azim and my dad are soul brothers to this day.

Azim had two children, Tariq and Tasreen. One morning we got a call. Tariq had been murdered. He was only twenty years old. Tariq was a college student with a job delivering pizza. As part of a gang initiation, a group of teenage wannabe gangbangers called in a fake pizza order. When Tariq refused to hand over the pizza, Tony Hicks, a fourteen-year-old, gunned him down.

The case got a lot of press. The gunman would be the youngest person ever tried for murder as an adult in California. Azim did something astounding. He forgave the shooter and spoke at trial on his behalf. He felt Tony was a victim too, of a society where kids had to find belonging in gangs. He implored the court to try Tony as a minor, but to no avail. Tony pled guilty as an adult and was sentenced to twenty-five years to life in prison.

When Tariq was murdered, my family became Azim's emotional crutch. Supporting our dear friend during the tragedy was the right thing to do. Unfortunately for our family unit, the loss of the hotel, my mom's loss of the theater when the hotel changed hands, and the emotional toll of helping Azim cope with his only son's murder started blowing my parents' marriage apart.

My dad needed to figure out what he was going to do with his life. He needed to grieve and find a path forward. His solution was to retreat to a solitary cabin in the mountains alone four days a week. He'd come home on Friday morning, spend the weekend with us, then take off for the mountains Monday morning.

Bless my mom. She stayed strong. Looking back, I can't imagine how hard it was on her. Like most youths, I was totally oblivious to anyone's feelings but my own. She was a rock, never downbeat, just kept on keeping on even though, as I learned later, she was completely torn apart.

After a long stretch, my dad came back and asked me if I'd like to go live near the beach where most of my school friends lived. I was going to a middle school in Point Loma, a San Diego beach community. I was thrilled by the idea. There was one catch. My mom wasn't coming with us. At age fourteen, this is how I found out that my parents were getting divorced.

I started drinking and abusing substances around age twelve. But when my parents officially got divorced and I went to live with my dad, things really went off the rails. Just about every day from age fourteen to twenty, I got stoned multiple times per day, including before school, and binge drank on the weekends. I became a burnout.

Train wreck that I was, I did have some redeeming qualities. I was smart, and I got good at relating to people and winning them over, from interacting with so many different types of people in the hotel.

I used these skills to cheat my way through middle school and high school. I made friends with kids who got good grades, and they let me copy their homework. In exchange for letting me copy their work, I gave my studious friends free weed and told them where they could buy beer as minors.

I took my SAT still drunk from the night before and somehow scored well enough to get into a college. Apparently, some of that stuff I'd copied was still hanging around in my brain. I went to college and earned good grades, even though the daily substance abuse continued.

I was kicked out of college during my junior year for disturbing the peace. Too much partying. Too much fighting and blatantly ignoring the rules. Not enough self-control. In truth, I felt I had nothing to live for—no purpose. I only got good grades because I didn't want to look like a loser to my friends.

Little did I know that the reason for turning my life around was waiting for me in Peru, of all places, where my dad and brother had started a new business a year and a half earlier. First, though, the college required me to do a stint in rehab if I wanted to return to school.

I spent two weeks in a downtown skid row detox center sweating it out with crack, heroin, and meth addicts. Going through rehab helped me a lot. I knew I didn't belong there and that I needed to change. The problem was I had no clue about who or what I needed to morph into.

CHAPTER 2

DAN

My dad, Dan, was born in Fort Wayne, Indiana, in 1939. His father, Victor, passed away from Hodgkin's disease at age thirty-three, when Dan was just four years old. Victor was the star and savior of his family, one of eight children raised by an abusive, alcoholic single father after their mother died. Victor singlehandedly led his clan out of destitution and breathed life into the family line. He became a trained chef and went on to open several restaurants called Vic's Diners, famous for their pies and homey midwestern hospitality. Just come on in, sit down, enjoy yourself. Have some pie and coffee and stay a while, you hear?

Vic was successful enough to buy himself an airplane, build an eleven-room house for his wife and kids, and give his siblings seed money to start their own businesses. They became a successful family of Indiana entrepreneurs, owners of restaurants and lumberyards.

When Victor died, the family was devastated. Their hero had fallen. Who was to lead the family now? Everybody started talking about four-year-old Danny as Vic's heir apparent. He was to be the next golden boy, the family's next great entrepreneur, as they figured any son of Vic Wick would have to be. Starting at age four, Danny planned to grow up and be like Vic. He wanted to get rich before the age of thirty-three, the age when Vic died. Secretly, Danny believed he might not live past that age himself.

Dan grew up playing basketball, baseball, and football. He was elected high school class president four years in a row, a first for any student at New Haven High. He was driven to succeed. He had a successful college career, graduating with top grades and serving as president of his fraternity. After graduating from college, Dan was accepted into and graduated from Naval Officer's Candidate School. He served during the Vietnam War on the USS *Ticonderoga*, an aircraft carrier.

While in the Navy, Dan fell in love for the first time. He and Nancy Curren met at a Christmas party while his ship was docked in San Diego. The two had a brief, passionate affair and made plans to elope after dating for only a few months.

Dan was scheduled to ship out soon and the idea of being separated without being married was too painful. At the last moment, Nancy revealed their wedding plans to her mother, and Nancy's mother persuaded her to wait. Young love turned to heartbreak. Dan shipped back off to war, unmarried, and the two went their separate ways.

After completing his naval service, Dan went to law school. He quickly realized he'd rather hire lawyers than be one. He switched to business and completed coursework for his master's degree. One of his business professors was working as a consultant putting together a pilot cattle investment project for a large company, and he asked Dan to work on the project with him.

After working on the project, Dan and a group of friends raised a round of capital and started their own cattle investment fund, one of the

first in the United States. After four years of making big money, a bro-
kerage firm wanted to take them public. Just as they were putting final
touches on the initial offering, President Nixon, confronted by raging
inflation, scotched their plans by freezing the price of beef without freezing the price of feed.

The partnership started losing a million dollars a month and was
wiped out within eighteen months. By age thirty-four, Dan's fortune had
dwindled to a modicum of cash that he literally stashed under his mattress. From flying high to nearly broke.

This was a devastating blow. Dan had planned to have children with
his love, Nancy, but the war prevented that. Instead, he showered all his
love and attention on the business. The business was his child, and now
it was dead.

In 1974, Dan and one of his partners used the money under the mattress
to buy and sell equipment parts that were in short supply during the infla-
tionary economy. Soon, the money grew into a small nest egg, enough
to fund a trip around the world. Over the next six months, Dan traveled
throughout Europe and Asia on a mission to grieve and discover what to
do next with his life.

While walking down the street in India, a yogi approached him out
of the blue, took him into a monastery, and revealed to him that learning to meditate was his ordained path. The yogi taught Dan traditional
Hindu transcendental meditation. Dan stayed with his teacher for three
days learning to meditate, then continued with his trip.

Once back in the United States, Dan felt compelled to continue with
his spiritual development. He spent eighteen months in an ashram in California. The ashram provided a stripped-down studio apartment, and rice
and vegetables to eat. The tenants meditated most of the day, ate together,
and received teaching from the ashram's gurus. After eighteen months of
meditation and simplicity, Dan felt ready to take on his future.

He headed back to San Diego with little money in the bank. It was the late 1970s. Dan was in his late thirties. Up to this point, his story had been one of loss. He'd lost his father young. He had lost the girl he loved. He'd made a bundle of money and lost it all. But through spiritual work and meditation, Dan had learned that loss is acceptable as long as you use it to evolve.

I've never studied the Hindu religion, but I grew up hearing about it from my dad. The essential tenet is that we are all souls going through a process of evolution. We live, die, and are reborn. If we lived well and evolved in our previous life, we'll have a better life in our next incarnation, filled with more control and more power. The process continues upward until a soul reaches a state of perfection and melds back into oneness with God.

This belief in the soul's evolution assuaged Dan's pain of loss. After all, if you believe in eternal evolution, what happens in this life is just one part of a much grander journey. Meditating twice a day, a practice he continues to this day, helped Dan get ready for his next adventure.

Driving home one day after a lunch meeting, Dan made a wrong turn and ended up in downtown San Diego's historic Gaslamp Quarter district. When he stumbled on the scene, downtown was in the early stages of redevelopment. There were plans for a massive new shopping mall next to the Gaslamp Quarter.

Dan saw opportunity. He networked with Gaslamp building owners and learned that there were tax credits for repairing and upgrading old buildings, but no banks were making those loans in the Gaslamp.

Dan became the district's finance officer for a year, convinced several banks to make loans, and discovered that the federal government was making second loans at very low rates to rehab old buildings. After a year, he started his own business, Gaslamp Quarter Enterprises.

Languishing on the site of the planned mall, a sole ghostly presence, was the Horton Grand Hotel, an historic landmark built in 1886. Everything else had been flattened. The Historical Society would not let it be taken down, and mall construction couldn't start until it was gone.

Staring at the hotel one day, Dan saw a solution—a most novel one. He could take the hotel apart brick by brick, piece by piece, and rebuild it on another site in the district. Dan brought the idea forward, and all parties bought into it. The Historical Society asked Dan if he would be willing to take down another 1886 hotel, where Wyatt Earp once had lived, and incorporate it into the project as well. Dan agreed.

Under Dan's supervision, with a state-issued bond, a loan from the city, and private investment capital, the old hotels were dismantled and artfully woven into the reconstructed Horton Grand Hotel. It reopened in 1986, on its hundredth anniversary, in the middle of the still decrepit and blighted district.

Early on in his Gaslamp saga, Dan was introduced to my mom, Kit Goldman. Kit was a producer and actress who had a theater company. She was smart, talented, driven, and beautiful. Her troupe was performing in small, rented venues downtown, and she wanted to build a theater of her own in the Gaslamp Quarter. Kit saw Dan as a good prospect to help her.

After they were introduced, as if by divine intervention, they started running into each other everywhere. They began dating and fell in love. Kit was a thirty-four-year-old single mother, with an eleven-year-old son, my brother, Brian. She had outgrown the relationship she was in and had all but given up on true love. As a symbol of her disillusionment, she'd had a tubal ligation, which made my birth an extreme long shot.

It was July of 1979 when Dan and Kit met. Six months later, with Dan wanting to experience life up close and personal in the Gaslamp

Quarter, he, Kit, and Brian all moved into the Grand Pacific Hotel, a beat-up Victorian flophouse that Dan and some partners had bought. After eight months with the colorful reprobates in the Grand Pacific, they moved into a house my dad owned and had been renting out in Golden Hill, the rough, rundown neighborhood adjacent to downtown where I would spend my younger years.

The two wanted a child together. Kit met with a doctor about reversing the tubal ligation. It was a long shot. The odds of her getting pregnant were just 10 percent. In 1982, sitting around the dinner table at her mother's house, Kit made the announcement. She was pregnant with a baby boy. Dan would become a father for the first time at age forty-three. Brian would be a big brother at age fourteen. Kit would have a second son.

CHAPTER 3

BRIAN

From a very young age, my brother, Brian Horsley, was forced to take on challenges. Our mom and Brian's father, Dave Horsley, were divorced when Brian was three. As a four-year-old, Brian flew frequently by himself from San Diego to Sacramento to visit his father. Visitation arrangements were that Brian would spend one weekend a month, and summers, with Dave.

This put Brian on airplanes, flying alone, nine to ten times a year. In the beginning, Brian had to lie about his age. The age requirement for flying alone then was five years old. When asked how old he was, Brian fibbed to get past the gate, hugged Mom goodbye, and flew off to see his father.

It wasn't only flying back and forth between cities as a little boy that taught Brian to be resourceful. Brian was primarily raised by our mom, Kit, one of the hardest charging, highest-energy people you will ever meet.

Kit's mother, Sybil, was a part-time actress and lover of the arts. Since childhood, Kit dreamed of putting on her own shows. Raising a son by herself wasn't going to keep her from chasing that dream. She began producing theater around town when Brian was six years old.

Being a single mother, Kit often brought Brian right along with her to the theater, exposing him to the freewheeling and flamboyant characters in the theater scene. Sometimes he was a latchkey kid, on his own, free to roam.

Kit and Brian lived at the beach. It was the era when skateboarding was breaking into the mainstream, a magical time for Brian and his buddies, who spent every minute they could skateboarding down the boardwalk or at pop-up skateparks.

Then, when Brian was eleven, Kit and my dad got together. Brian not only had a new stepfather, but he was forced to say goodbye to the beach and say hello to their new home in a fleabag downtown hotel. He traded knee boarding on the boardwalk, side by side with the Pacific Ocean, for riding his bicycle down skid row, side by side with junkies.

Instead of starting junior high school with his elementary school buddies in a laid-back beach environment, Brian enrolled, friendless, in what was then one of the most rugged urban schools in the city, Roosevelt Junior High.

Coming into Brian's teenage years, it was decided that the living arrangements with his mom and dad would be reversed. Kit figured it would be healthy for a teenage boy to spend more time with his father. Brian would live with Dave full time and visit Kit and Dan one weekend a month and summers.

Brian was now forced to adapt to his father's rapidly changing conditions. Dave Horsley moved around a lot. When Brian entered ninth grade, Dave, a nature lover, decided to buy land in rural Idaho.

Brian started at a new high school in ninth grade, the first of three high schools he would attend before flunking out in the twelfth grade.

In Idaho, Dave decided to test his hand at entrepreneurship, and he brought Brian in as a junior partner. Dave went to taxidermy school and learned how to stuff dead animals.

Folks were hunting enthusiasts in Idaho, and it seemed like there would be a decent clientele. The two built out an office, bought all the gear, and hung up their shingle. Brian went to school during the day and helped his dad with taxidermy in the afternoons and evenings.

A huge recession hit during their first year in business. Hunters decided to save money by staying home. Dave couldn't make rent or service the loans he'd taken out to get the business going. While Brian was in San Diego for the summer, Dave made the decision to flee Idaho for his brother's home in Fresno, California.

When summer ended, Brian learned he would not be going back to Idaho, but to Fresno. He'd start at a new school in the fall, again. In Fresno, Brian found his father in bad shape in every way imaginable. Dave had failed at business, he was broken, and he didn't know what to do next. I saw my dad go through the same struggle, so I can easily imagine what that was like.

In Fresno, Brian's grades started to slip. He had finally reached a level in school that required some real effort. Before that, Brian had always skated by on superior natural intelligence.

As most dads would do, Dave started ragging on Brian, telling him over and over that he needed to get his act together. Brian ignored his father, and instead of buckling down and working harder, he went in the opposite direction, focusing less on school and more on drugs and partying.

After two years in Fresno, Brian was informed over the summer that his dad had taken a new job in Long Beach, California. Brian would be forced to switch high schools yet again, this time for his senior year. Years of change and moving and struggle culminated in Brian abandoning any pretense that he cared about school. Substance abuse spiked dramatically, and he was on the verge of becoming a high school dropout and drug addict.

In the throes of Brian's breakdown, Dave had a come-to-Jesus meeting with him and suggested that he join the army. Dave made a heartfelt apology for his shortcomings as a parent and told Brian that there weren't any better options. Brian views this as Dave's best parenting moment.

Dave admitted his own mistakes and gave Brian guidance that could put him on the best track available.

In a last-ditch effort, driven by how much he'd let everybody down, Brian completed his course work to graduate during summer school, after which he enlisted in the army and headed to basic training in Georgia.

In the army, Brian learned work ethic, teamwork, and how to follow rules. He got the structure that had been missing from his life. He learned how to fight, use weapons, and be an acute observer of his environment.

After three years in the military, Brian moved back to San Diego and enrolled in City College with his GI bill. He moved in with roommates and worked as a valet at the Horton Grand Hotel. Two years later, after earning an associate degree, Brian decided to study political science at San Diego State University. However, the California State University system was in a budget crisis. There were staffing shortages, and Brian couldn't get the classes he needed.

So, he did what any normal person would do: loaded up his bags and went backpacking throughout Southeast Asia for a year. His trip took him to Thailand, Vietnam, Cambodia, and many other places. Picking up and taking off on an adventure like that comes naturally for Brian and me, the children of entrepreneurs.

After the trip, Brian assessed his options and decided to finish his studies at the University of California Riverside where they had the classes for his major. Brian graduated two years later with straight As and moved back to San Diego.

He came back to a very different scene in San Diego than the one he had left three years earlier. Dad's very public loss of the hotel, and Mom her theater, had taken a huge emotional toll. Their marriage was falling apart. I was eleven years old, listening to gangster rap all the time and failing miserably in school. Our friend Azim's son had been murdered.

Brian's army training, education, and maturation from traveling abroad prepared him to step in and help. He took over as executive director of the Tariq Khamisa Foundation, a nonprofit organization Azim had launched in honor of his son.

After a good stretch at the foundation, managing fundraising drives and teaching at-risk, inner-city kids how to avoid violence, Brian decided it was time to move on.

Brian signed on as a project manager overseeing installation of high-speed internet in big office buildings across the country. Being on the road, meeting clients, overseeing installation teams, problem solving, and building and fostering relationships to grow revenue were all things Brian did extremely well.

During this period, Brian was in a steady, long-term relationship with someone he cared for deeply. He was making very good money. Yet something was nagging at him deep within his soul. He had an entrepreneurial spirit, and the idea of working at a big company as an employee for the rest of his life tormented him. Brian quit his job and decided to chase his entrepreneurial dream.

My dad describes the years after losing his hotel as crossing the bankruptcy desert. He knew it would be impossible for him to get financing or raise a round of equity until he rebuilt his credit. He also knew with absolute certainty that he would start another business as soon as he could. He just had to bide his time.

When I graduated from high school in 2001, my dad had finally crossed the desert. He announced to me triumphantly one afternoon that he was getting back in the game.

He was a sixty-two-year-old man who hadn't done business in quite a while. His previous two businesses were roller-coaster rides that ultimately failed. Yet there he was, brimming with enthusiasm and confidence, ready to jump back on the roller coaster to see where it would take him. My dad has done many things to make me proud. He's lived a rich life filled with unique achievements. But the moment when he told me he was going for it again made me prouder than just about anything else.

CHAPTER 4
PERU

The idea of going to Peru or living in Peru never would have crossed our minds. We had no previous connection to Peru and had never thought of Peru for any reason. I'm certain that I couldn't have pointed out Peru on a map. Yet we were Peru-bound.

When Dad came out of bankruptcy, Brian quit his job, and they decided to go into business together. Brian worked nights as a bartender to make ends meet while they figured out what kind of business to start. They had no idea whatsoever what they were going to do. They only knew that they wanted to do it together.

They read public lists of recently granted patents. They researched different industries. They scoured Dun and Bradstreet. They talked to the chamber of commerce. They networked with the local branch of the World Trade Organization. They shook every tree and looked under every rock trying to find an opportunity they believed in.

After nine months of strenuous research, they found it: air filter cleaners. You read that right, air filter cleaners. My dad had waited seven long, grueling years to come out of bankruptcy. This was to be his final grasp at glory. And what did they decide to pursue? Again, air filter cleaners.

I came home from college during winter break that year and was accosted by Dad and Brian. They excitedly sat me down on the couch to watch a video. They slid the VHS into the VCR (remember those?) and made me watch a promotional video about air filter cleaners. Once the video was over, they asked me what I thought. I told them that I had absolutely no idea what they were trying to tell me.

They laid it out. Mines—for example, gold mines—deploy behemoth trucks that haul hundreds of tons of dirt per trip. It's a very dusty business. Air filters keep dust from getting into the motor and destroying the cylinders. On such a big truck, the air filters are very big and very expensive. Given the constant dustiness of the work, air filters need to be replaced frequently.

The technology that Dan and Brian were so excited about alleviated the problem of having to replace air filters. With a simple little attachment to a truck, mine maintenance departments could cut a huge percentage off the time spent replacing air filters. Mines could also pocket tremendous savings by reducing the number of air filters that needed to be purchased.

Dan and Brian had spoken with the manufacturer and worked out a deal. The manufacturer would grant them exclusive selling privileges to any mine they signed up. The air filter cleaner was a new technology with patents, and the manufacturer agreed to never sell directly to the customers we brought on board.

There was just one teensy, tiny, little problem to overcome. None of us had any idea how to sell stuff to a mine. Thankfully, Azim Khamisa, the dear friend whom our family had rallied around, knew someone who could help us. Azim introduced Dan to a consultant named Steve Feher. Steve had a contract with Newmont, a mining company based out of Colorado.

Newmont owned and operated Minera Yanacocha, the biggest gold mine in the world at that time, measured by volume of production. Minera Yanacocha is located outside of a mountain town in northern Peru called Cajamarca. Steve was working on-site in Cajamarca.

Azim arranged a phone meeting, and Dan pitched Steve on the air filter cleaners. Steve found it interesting and agreed to discuss it with the supervisor of truck maintenance at Minera Yanacocha. The supervisor was an American who had just started working at the mine. He found the air-filter-cleaner concept interesting too, and agreed to meet with Dan at the mine.

Just like that, we had our foot in the door with a mining company. And it wasn't just any mining company. These were the folks who owned and operated the biggest gold mine in the entire world. They had hundreds and hundreds of huge, heavy load trucks. Those trucks kicked up a lot of dust and dirtied a lot of filters.

On that first trip, Steve Feher was waiting in the Lima airport to take Dan to Cajamarca. They walked out on the tarmac and saw dozens of nice, modern planes with thousands of passengers boarding. Steve informed Dan that those planes were flying to Cusco, the famous Incan capital, home of Machu Picchu, Peru's number one tourist attraction.

A tiny prop plane pulled up. Dan, Steve, and thirteen other passengers climbed aboard to take a flight from the central Peruvian coast to a small mountain town tucked away in the northern Peruvian Andes.

As you approach, Cajamarca appears like an oasis hidden behind a never-ending stretch of jagged, barren ridges. You want to rub your eyes to make sure it's real. It seems marvelous and magical that human beings could build a city as vibrant and charming as Cajamarca in such a remote location. Yet there it is, a testament to human ingenuity and endurance.

Because of the high altitude, nine thousand feet, Dan was instructed upon arrival to drink coca tea and rest for a day in his hotel to avoid altitude sickness. The hotel was located on the perimeter of Cajamarca's Plaza de Armas.

The concept of a *plaza de armas* is a relic of Spanish imperialism. The Spanish administrations in South and Central America tended to lay out their cities on a grid, with a town square in the middle. The word *armas* translates to "weapons," and the original purpose of a plaza de armas was to give the town militia a place to bunker down and gather weapons in case of an invasion. Since wars weren't raging all the time, plazas became centers of town cultural life.

Dan sat on the balcony of his hotel overlooking the Plaza de Armas, wondering what would come of this adventure. He was taken aback by this little city that offered such a stark mixture of very old and very new. The mine was bringing in folks from all over the world, like himself, looking to do business in Cajamarca.

Minera Yanacocha was generating tremendous economic prosperity for Cajamarca's educated class. There was an insatiable need for engineers and financial analysts. On the other hand, there was the preexisting local culture, that of a sleepy, old mountain town inhabited by families who tracked their lineage back for centuries.

This all led to a mishmash of traditional and modern. Brand-new pickup trucks and motorcycles zoomed around the plaza. Mine employees in designer jeans and expensive leather shoes strolled through town, their well-dressed, well-off families in tow.

Meanwhile, *campesinos*, traditional country farmers who lived off the land in the surrounding mountains, hoofed through town in their open-toed leather sandals, straw hats, and typical multicolored, yellow, green, red, and pink Alpaca skirts and ponchos, heavy loads of hay or herbs on their backs, behind herds of cattle or sheep, faces deeply tanned from working outdoors. In between classic old churches were new stores selling refrigerators and washing machines.

After a day of rest and acclimation to the altitude, Dan left early the next morning to visit the mine. He was picked up by Steve Feher in a four-wheel drive pickup truck, and they headed out.

A couple of hours later, Dan was on-site at the mine to discuss air filter cleaners with the new American truck-maintenance supervisor. It only took fifteen minutes to find out that air filter cleaners were a nonstarter. Refitting hundreds of trucks was too big of a project and a pilot wasn't cost effective. Nine months of research down the drain in fifteen minutes.

However, something else came up in the discussion. The supervisor wanted an alternative supplier of hydraulic hoses and certain types of nuts and bolts. The only products then available were from Caterpillar through their national distributor in Peru, a huge company called Ferreyros.

Everybody in the maintenance department knew that Ferreyros was price gouging and that lower cost options were available. The mine supervisor gave Dan the name of several companies in the United States who sold the exact products needed much cheaper than CAT and Ferreyros.

The supervisor knew for certain these other companies had no distributors in Peru. If Dan could get those products to the mine for a lower price than Caterpillar, the mine would buy them. Dan said he was interested, and wanted to discuss it with his partner before giving a response. In Dan's mind, this deal was already done.

The World Bank owned 5 percent of the mine, and one of the requirements when you take World Bank money is that the project has to buy a certain percentage of supplies from local vendors. This was supposed to stimulate the local economy and give back some of the wealth.

Steve told Dan that it would be hell competing with Ferreyros and Caterpillar head-to-head. Mine workers could be influenced through graft and relationships to choose higher cost CAT products.

Steve suggested that Dan team up with local businesses to distribute to the mine. This would give management an incentive to enforce the use of our products. Not only would the prices be better, but the use of our products would allow the mine to comply with an important regulatory requirement.

Dan asked Steve if he knew any local businesses in Cajamarca who would want to participate in the project. Steve said he knew several.

Dan agreed to go back to the United States and work with Brian to lock down relationships with the manufacturers. Steve promised to discuss the opportunity with local business owners he knew.

Back in the United States, Dan shared the results of his trip with Brian. After nine months of research, Brian was ready for action. Dan reached back out to the mine supervisor and got contact information for the manufacturers.

Brian and Dan used what little money they had in their bank accounts to fly around the country learning how to buy and export hydraulic hoses and nuts and bolts. They drew up purchasing agreements with manufacturers that allowed for extremely competitive pricing, 30 to 40 percent lower than CAT prices in most cases.

Steve Feher lined up interviews with local Cajamarcan business owners. A few months after Dan's first trip, he and Brian scheduled a trip to Peru together to finalize the deals needed to start the project.

Prior to knowing where the research for the new business would take him, Brian was essentially just a bartender, a nondescript thirtysomething, trying to make his way in the world. He had quit his corporate job and was chasing a dream, but he didn't have much to show for it. While he was tending bar and talking to customers, he could throw out that he was starting a business. The customers might nod politely and mechanically ask a few questions. But people starting a business are a dime a dozen. Starting a business doesn't mean it's going anywhere. However, when you tell people you're flying to Peru on business next week, the equation changes. That is real and tangible, and Peru sounds so exotic.

In Cajamarca, Brian was a complete rarity. He was a relatively young and handsome American businessman who could speak the local language. He had picked up Spanish talking to the restaurant and maintenance staff at the Horton Grand, and the kitchen crew at the hotel where he bartended. He relished immersing himself in the local culture, getting away from the Plaza de Armas, and walking around in neighborhoods where nonmine folks lived and worked. He could hobnob with mine executives as well as charm the local business owners who would become our partners.

Women followed Brian in the street and catcalled him, something you don't see much in the United States but that is common in Peru. By the time the first trip was over, Brian was looking at himself in a completely different light.

In Cajamarca, Brian and Dan came to agreements with two local businesses. One was Automotriz Cajamarca, a thriving auto repair shop, owned by Segundo Sandoval, a successful and eccentric businessman. Segundo had bid on, and won, a big contract to do maintenance for mine-owned pickup trucks.

Our second local partner was a company called FISAC, owned by the Carranza family. Compared to Segundo Sandoval, the Carranzas were old money. Brian and Dan met with Francisco Carranza, patriarch of the sprawling, family-owned conglomerate. The Carranzas controlled industrial supply and shipping interests throughout Peru. Brian was advised by Steve Feher not to do any talking in the meeting. Steve explained that it is traditional in Peru for patriarchs to negotiate with one another. It is disrespectful for a son to butt into business dealings when two fathers are talking. Dan and Francisco hit it off famously.

Almost everything was in place now. The company would distribute nuts and bolts through Automotriz Cajamarca and hydraulic hoses through FISAC. Dan and Brian would go back and forth between the United States and Peru to manage the project.

They worked feverishly to get a proposal to the mine before the trip ended. A week later, the mine sent a three-year contract to purchase up to $6 million worth of parts, contingent on usage. The contract also included a purchase order of $500,000 for initial stock. A year after Brian quit his corporate job to team up with Dan, they were officially in business.

CHAPTER 5

EXPULSION

While my dad and Brian were working hard getting a new business off the ground, I was expelled from college and had to go to rehab.

When I came back from school and walked into my dad's two-bedroom apartment, he sat me down at the dining room table and said we needed to have a talk. He looked me in the eyes. It was a long, intense stare. Finally, he broke the silence.

"You're spoiled. You're ruining your life. You have no idea how good and easy you have it. You need to see how other people live. You're going to Peru this summer."

I told him that I had to go through rehab if I wanted to get back into school. He told me that I'd better make plans to do that as soon as possible. Once I was done with the program, I was to pack my bags and head out immediately.

I told him that I didn't have the money to pay for rehab. He said I better find a way to make some because he sure as hell wasn't going to pay for it. He added that I should make some extra money to take to Peru. The job he had lined up for me there wasn't going to pay well.

At the hotel where my brother tended bar, the general manager helped me out with a short-term job as a banquet waiter. I worked hard, earned a couple thousand bucks, then checked myself into rehab.

The rehab experience was profound—one of the most important and enlightening experiences of my life. It showed me that I had a terrible problem with perspective. In my mind, I had big problems and had lived a hard life. I came to realize how miniscule my suffering was compared to what my rehab roommates were facing.

I realized that if I didn't change course, my problems would grow into their problems. Thankfully, there was still a way out for me. Unlike my roomies, I had opportunities beyond jail and street life. Golden opportunities. Not only school. I was about to go to Peru.

CHAPTER 6

THE GOLD MINE

With the contract signed, Brian arranged the first shipment of hoses and hardware. This meant learning a bunch of new things with which he had zero experience. This is Brian's wheelhouse.

How are hydraulic hoses and nuts and bolts packaged? How do you ship them to a port from the manufacturer and get them on a boat? Which port? What kind of customs paperwork is needed? How do you get through customs in Peru? How do you get everything off a boat in Lima and onto a truck for Cajamarca? How do you get all this stuff delivered to the mine? How do we get people to use our products instead of the competitor's?

Before Brian and Dan knew it, they were back in Cajamarca welcoming their first container of product. It had taken several months to make it happen, but time flew in the whirlwind leading up to the big moment.

Brian triumphantly followed two freight trucks from Cajamarca into the mine's receiving area, where he filled out the receiving paperwork. He oversaw a team of hired workers as they unloaded our precious inventory into bins that the maintenance department had designated for us.

The mine's maintenance department is twelve thousand feet above sea level. It can be a cold, windy, lonely place. After the products were delivered, the paperwork was signed, and everything was put into bins, the workers left, and Brian was alone.

He stood by himself and looked around the storage room filled with parts. It occurred to him that he hadn't been paid for this venture yet. He had left his high-paying job well over a year earlier. He was still tending bar to make ends meet and would be for the foreseeable future. The company wouldn't be paid by the mine for more than ninety days. That was the earliest Brian could potentially draw his first paycheck from the company, almost a year and half after getting started. The company couldn't make another sale until most of the current shipment was used up. No telling how long that would take.

From the United States, Brian reviewed usage reports from our Peruvian partners. When he was in Cajamarca and on-site at the mine, the numbers rose dramatically. When he was back in the States, the numbers fell off a cliff. It was easy enough to do the math and realize that if Brian lived in Cajamarca full time, the company could go through product fast enough for Brian to draw a full paycheck.

Seeing this as the only logical path forward for the business, Brian made plans to move down to Peru. More than two years after leaving his cushy corporate gig to start a business, Brian was able to quit bartending. The only caveat: he had to live in a foreign country to get paid.

The move was good for the business, but bad for an important part of Brian's personal life. He had been in a good, strong relationship for almost ten years, but the relationship had come under strain. Brian's previous road job, and the current business, had taken a toll.

Brian and his lady decided to move down to Peru together as a last-ditch effort to save the relationship. After a six-month try, with their hearts hurting, the couple split up. Brian's fiancée headed back to the United States, and Brian soldiered on by himself in Cajamarca.

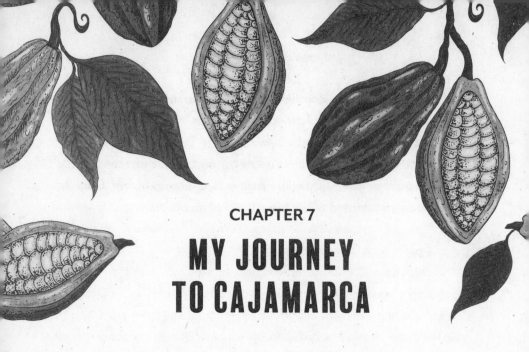

CHAPTER 7

MY JOURNEY TO CAJAMARCA

O n the afternoon I left rehab, I went to my dad's apartment and learned about my itinerary. I'd fly into Lima early the next morning, then take a fifteen-hour bus ride from Lima to Cajamarca.

I was a Spanish major in college and could read and write Spanish well, but couldn't speak or understand it if spoken to. I had a piece of paper with two addresses on it. I was to show the paper to a taxi driver at the airport to get to the bus station in Lima. Once in Cajamarca, I'd show the second address to another taxi driver to get from the bus station to the apartment where my brother would be waiting for me.

Early the next morning, my dad drove me to the airport, dropped me off, gave me a hug, and drove away. I'd never been out of the country before, and flying internationally was a whole new thing for me. I asked around at the airport about what I was supposed to do, and finally, there I was, buckled up, super excited, admittedly nervous, heading for the unknown in Peru.

I traveled all day and overnight and showed up in Lima early the next day. After filling out customs paperwork, I got my luggage, changed some money, and headed out to find a taxi.

The taxi drivers in the airport lobby fell on travelers in a thick mass, making it hard to move through. I kept wading forward, determined to get outside. I didn't want to hire a taxi until I had my bearings, made sure I had all my luggage, and double-checked that I still had the all-important piece of paper with the addresses.

Outside I waved a taxi driver over and showed him the paper. He gave me a thumbs-up and carried my luggage to a beat-up old Toyota Camry. I climbed into the back seat and noticed that the upholstery was split apart from wear and tear. We passed through a security booth and took off into the streets of Lima.

I stared out the window at the gray, overcast sky and fell into a trance as the blocks floated by. The driver tried to spark up a conversation, but I wasn't in the right frame of mind to converse. I politely told him, "No Español."

What struck me was how big Lima was. At that time, it was a city of nine million people. It's even bigger now. We drove and drove. The city felt endless. The world became much bigger and I much smaller during that drive.

After the long trip through the city, we made it to the bus station. My seat was on the upper level of a double-decker bus. My wonderful brother had booked me all the way up front where there was a large lookout window. I had the best seat in the house for the long, mind-bending trip up the coast and into the mountains.

After roughly 450 miles driving north up the coast, just past the beach city of Pacasmayo, we'd be turning east to climb into the Andes. One road would take us on our entire journey north, route 1N, the Pan-Americana.

The Pan-Americana is a thick road, running through the middle of tiny towns. From the bus, I saw old women in the street grilling meat in front of their small homes. I saw groups of men sitting around tables in front of shops drinking beer. I saw kids playing soccer out in dry, brown fields. Groups of women, young and old, played volleyball in the street. The houses were concrete or brick. There were gardens with tall corn stalks poking out above the tops of short wire fences. Dogs ran free, chasing the bus as it drove by. The Pacific Ocean was ever present on the western horizon, but not always in view.

Traveling up the coast, under the night sky, I saw nothing. No houses. No cities. No lights. An eerie nothingness. The coast had transformed into a vast, barren desert with the ocean on its perimeter.

Every hour or so, we'd drive through a city built on a river running down from the Andes into the sea. Cities in this desert must be near a river to exist. Then, as fast as we'd entered the city, we'd come out the other side and be greeted by more emptiness.

Some of the bigger coastal cities like Chimbote, Trujillo, and Chiclayo have enough water from rivers and subterranean water supplies to irrigate the coastal desert and maintain gigantic farming operations. Sugar cane is especially prevalent.

In Trujillo, I saw a second major Peruvian city up close. Trujillo is famous for many things, including the Marinera Norteña, the iconic dance of northern Peru. Outside of Trujillo is one of the most breathtaking archeological sites in the world, Chan Chan, with its huge protective walls.

Two hours north of Trujillo, we drove past Pacasmayo, a lovely beach town, and crossed over the robust Jequetepeque River. On the other side of the river, we turned east onto Highway 8.

Highway 8 is for the most part a narrow, two-lane road that works its way up into the Andes Mountains. In the mountains, the bus started switching back and forth in heart-stopping earnest. Up on the second deck, I couldn't see the road. We were driving next to steep hills that descended into valleys far below. There were guardrails on the side of the road, but nothing that would keep a double-decker bus from tumbling off and rolling downhill until it disintegrated.

There were tiny adobe houses sprinkled across the open, grassy landscape. Here, folks lived off the land. Their land was what sustained them. They farmed. They raised cattle and other livestock. There were no amenities. No ninety-inch flat-screen TVs. No Costcos or Walmarts or Targets or Teslas. No drive-through Starbucks or car washes or gas stations.

For a kid to go to school meant a several-mile hike along Highway 8, through the countryside, to the nearest little town. I saw kids making that trek through the mountains with no adult supervision.

Most of the women wore traditional attire—skirts, blouses, hats, woolen shawls, and hard-soled shoes or leather sandals. Sometimes those woolen shawls were wrapped around a baby on a mother's back, or used to carry sticks, herbs, or crops.

Donkeys and horses with harnesses draped over their backs carried silver canisters filled with milk. This was the heart of the famous Cajamarca cheese industry. Farmers taking their milk to the nearest cheese processing facility, unfailingly made a several-mile hike in each direction. I was in a world I never knew existed. The first of many.

I wanted to take it all in, tried not to sleep, but finally dozed off. I awoke as we pulled into the Cajamarca bus station about nine in the morning. I walked with my bags into a crowd of taxis, trying to keep my coursing adrenaline under wraps, and chose a driver. He loaded my bags, I showed him my treasured paper with the address, and off we went into the streets of Cajamarca. I couldn't believe I was finally there.

When we arrived at the address, I whipped up my courage and asked the driver, "Cuanto?" ("How much?"). He said, "Cinco," and showed me five fingers. I fiddled around with coins and found one with the number five on it. He gave me a thumbs-up and took the coin.

I later learned that the legal price for a taxi between any two points in town was two *soles*, not five. The taxi driver had taken advantage of me. As time went on, I took great pleasure in busting taxi drivers trying to jack up the price on me.

CHAPTER 8

BROS IN PERU

Brian and my dad were renting a two-bedroom apartment roughly ten blocks uphill from the Plaza de Armas. I lugged my bags up a flight of stairs and knocked on the apartment door. The moment Brian answered, we shouted with joy, hugged each other, and jumped around in circles.

After the euphoria settled down, I looked up and saw somebody else standing in the apartment. He had thick, black hair, a bushy, black mustache, and thick-rimmed glasses. Brian introduced me to Segundo Sandoval, my new boss.

"Mucho gusto! Bienvenido!" exclaimed Segundo smiling. He came in close and gave me a warm hug.

"Mucho gusto" and "bienvenido" are two of the most fundamental Spanish phrases a person can learn. I had two years of college-level Spanish education, yet I had to turn to my brother for translation.

"What did he say?" I asked.

"He said, 'Mucho gusto,' nice to meet you, and, 'Bienvenido,' welcome. You need to listen more carefully, bro," responded Brian.

"Gracias," I said to Segundo with a little bow.

After stowing my luggage, Brian said we were going out to buy work clothes in the market. My dad had arranged for me to work as an auto mechanic in Segundo's garage. I would start my new job the very next day. Segundo was coming along to tell us what to buy.

The market looked to me like a gigantic swap meet. There were tables and stalls as far as the eye could see. In one stall, there was an elderly campesino woman wearing a tall straw hat, sitting on a short stool among barrels of uncooked rice and beans. In the next stall, a folding table covered in children's socks and underwear. On and on it went.

A group of teeny-bopper Peruvian kids pointed at me and guffawed. I looked back at them, pointed to myself, and raised my eyebrows to inquire silently if it was me they were laughing at. They nodded yes, affirming the obvious.

I caught up to Brian and tapped him on the shoulder. Like a real wuss, I told him that a bunch of kids were laughing at me. Was I doing something wrong?

"Look at yourself and look around," said Brian. "You're a freak of nature around here. You're a big, old, tall, six-foot four-inch, gangly, goofy white guy. You don't speak the language. People are going to point and laugh and follow you around the entire time you're here. You'll have to get used to it."

I looked back at the kids and gave them a thumbs-up. They shouted, "Bye-bye, gringo!" and laughed their heads off. Youngsters yelling English words at me was to become a regular occurrence.

We came to a stall that sold the one-piece coveralls mechanics wear to protect their clothing. The person working the stall told us in no uncertain terms that it would be impossible to find coveralls in my size. He advised that we buy the biggest size available and accept that the legs and arms would be short. Brian thought that over for a second and told me to try on the coveralls to see how they fit.

Right there in the middle of the market, I put on the coveralls. I didn't want to because I figured it would draw a crowd, but I complied as little brothers usually do. Sure enough, about six inches of leg and four inches of arm were left exposed. Also, sure enough, a group of onlookers stood around watching the giant gringo try on clothing that was far too small.

Brian and Segundo agreed that the coveralls were good enough, and a price negotiation ensued. I tried to shimmy out of the coveralls, but it wasn't easy. They fit so tightly, I had to wrestle them off. By the time I was done, I was red from exertion, and my hair was ridiculous. The crowd got quite a nice little show.

We closed the deal on the coveralls then went looking for work boots in my size. After an hour, we miraculously found one shoe salesman with a big enough boot. He jacked up the price when he saw who the boots were for, which hurt, because I knew I'd have to pay Brian back for the purchase.

In the afternoon, Brian showed me how to walk from our apartment to Automotriz Cajamarca, where I'd be working. It was a thirty-minute walk, about twenty blocks. I'd have to make that walk early in the morning to get to work by 8:00 AM. Then I'd have to walk back to the house for lunch. Then back to the garage after lunch. Then back to the house again at 6:00 PM when the workday was over.

CHAPTER 9

GRINGO ON THE CREW

The next day, I woke up early and put on my coveralls. Not knowing there was a locker room at the shop where everyone changed into work garb, I walked twenty blocks through town in my ill-fitting coveralls.

When I arrived, a group of young men who looked to be in their early twenties, like me, milled around out front next to a thick metal double door locked with a heavy chain.

A short, wise-looking fellow with curly black hair and dark brown eyes took pity on me and introduced himself. His name was Lucho. The others followed suit, gathering around to tell me their names and give me friendly handshakes. Conversation broke out, and everyone started joking around, as groups of young men do. I listened hard and picked up a few words.

Eventually, Segundo arrived and unlocked the big front door. We all headed to the locker room where everyone but me took out their work gear, changed, and bantered. I stood and watched.

A few minutes later, we headed out to the workstations. The supervisor, a stocky man with glasses, motioned for me to follow him to a pickup truck with the hood popped open. Step by step, he showed me how to change an oil filter.

"Entiendes?" he asked me. I didn't know that *entender* was another verb for "understand." I had only learned *comprender* in school. I looked at him, confused. After a few tries he resorted to a thumbs-up and a questioning look. This I understood, and I returned the thumbs-up. From that point forward, I'd be the guy changing oil filters on all the trucks.

In the afternoon, the supervisor taught me how to rotate tires. Once he saw that I picked it up, tire rotations were added to my responsibilities. I earned everybody's respect that first day. They saw I wasn't just some spoiled gringo on vacation. I knew how to work.

Six PM was closing time. I changed with the gang into clothes I'd brought during my lunch break and left my work gear in a locker. Cajamarca was a wonderland at twilight. I came to love walking home after work, tired, with oil all over my hands.

After my first day of work, I got up the courage to take a long route home. Instead of walking straight to our apartment, I walked the street leading to the Plaza de Armas.

The sky had dimmed but was not yet dark. Mountains were still barely visible outside of town. Food carts had been wheeled out, and the smell of sizzling meat filled the air. The street was packed with happy people who were done working for the day. They were loose and cordial, free and joking. Music was coming from somewhere, maybe everywhere.

The main road to the Plaza de Armas had shops and restaurants and old churches with parishioners sitting in courtyards out front. I peered into the restaurants and saw families sharing meals.

Every night, hundreds of people gathered in the Plaza de Armas to sit and talk or stroll around. Little kids sprinted carelessly and rolled in the grass while parents sat on park benches smiling, then scolding. Teenagers gathered in groups, sharing secrets in hushed tones followed by bursts of laughter. Old folks sat quietly and pondered. Groups of men sat on concrete walls alongside the shallow staircases that led down to the fountain in the center of the plaza.

I decided to do a couple of laps around the Plaza de Armas before heading home. My hope was to walk casually and observe nighttime in Cajamarca. I was so caught up in the magic that I forgot what an oddity I was. I was soon reminded.

Kids still in school uniforms followed me, giggling. Girls and young women made kissing sounds as I walked by. My face turned red. People stopped talking midconversation and pointed at me. Others whispered and nodded in my direction. Everyone stared. I spent my laps waving, smiling, and bowing apologetically as if to say, "I'm sorry. I know. I'm tall. I'm white. I'm goofy. Please feel free to look and laugh." After my laps, I made the ten-block hike uphill to our apartment.

Toward the end of my second day at work, several coworkers gathered around me. They had a question to ask me that was weighing heavily on their minds. They wanted to know what we ate for lunch in the United States. They had to repeat the question to me slowly several times. Finally, I understood and told them that we mostly ate sandwiches.

They couldn't believe it.

"Sandwiches?" they asked.

"Yes, we eat sandwiches," I replied.

"Every day?" they asked.

"Yes, I eat sandwiches for lunch almost every day," I said in choppy Spanish.

They had looks of disbelief and disappointment on their faces. That wasn't what they wanted to hear. The crowd broke up, apparently dejected by my answer, and everybody went back to work, except Lucho.

Lucho looked curiously into my face. I was more than a foot taller than he was. He stood close and had to bend his neck back to get a look at me.

Lucho was my age, but put off the energy of an old sage. He grabbed my bicep softly and asked if I would like to come to his house for lunch the next day. He told me that his mother would cook for us. I told him that I'd love to.

When lunchtime on my third day in town came around, I took off my coveralls, said goodbye to the gang, and followed Lucho home. We were an odd couple, Lucho and I, walking through the streets of Cajamarca. He was taking me to a neighborhood I never would have visited on my own.

Lucho and his mother lived in one of the poorest parts of the city. As we got farther away from Automotriz Cajamarca, near the outskirts of town, the neighborhoods became increasingly less developed. The roads were dirt. The houses were brick and adobe, almost no concrete. The children were barefoot, with sooty faces, ragged clothes, and unbrushed hair.

We came upon a big open field with several dozen houses lined up on a grid. The land had been leveled and covered with dirt and pebbles. Small plots had been sold, and families built simple, tiny houses on their plots. The houses were almost entirely gray brick with tin roofs. There was just enough space between the houses for people to walk through and for a door to open. The makeshift neighborhood was surrounded by enormous, brown mountains.

I followed Lucho down a narrow path through the grid to his house. When we entered, I was surprised to see just how small the houses really were. Lucho lived in a single room with his mother.

The house had a dirt floor. Lucho's mother had a bed pushed up against one of the gray walls. Lucho slept in a loft above his mother's bed. The loft was bolted to the wall and had tall, strong, wooden legs supporting it.

In the middle of the room was a wooden table that Lucho proudly told me he'd built himself. Along either side of the table were wooden benches. In the corner of the room, Lucho's mother was finishing lunch for us.

Her prep counter was a folding plastic table with cutting boards on top. It was covered in chopped onions, tomatoes, herbs, and chicken bones. Her stove was what an American would call a camp stove, propped up on cinder blocks, with a propane tank on the floor below.

Lucho's mother came to greet me. She motioned for me to lean in so that she could give me a kiss on the cheek. This is local custom when you greet a woman. I reached out to shake her hand after the kiss, but she showed me that her hands were dirty.

Lucho greeted his mother, and she kissed him on the cheek as well. They paused for a moment to look at each other. Lucho loved his mother. His face showed deep appreciation and respect. She was clearly proud of her boy, who had studied to become an auto mechanic, and who worked hard to support them. She beamed at him with a warm smile and motioned for us to sit down. The room smelled wonderful. We sat and ate, and the food was the best I'd ever tasted.

After lunch, I slouched with my forearms on the table, full. Lucho leaned in close, and with a mischievous smirk, he said, "Better than sandwiches, right?" I broke into a loud laugh and said, "Sandwiches, nunca mas!" ("Sandwiches, never again!") Lucho and his mother laughed along with me.

When it was time to leave, I thanked our wonderful hostess to the best of my ability. On our way out, I looked around and realized there was no sink, just several buckets of water. This was a hardworking woman who had raised a good son. In truth, her son was a better man than I was at that moment in time.

Walking back, a philosophical breakthrough raged in my head. How does somebody with all the opportunity in the world, lucky enough to spend half his life in a hotel his dad owned, who goes to a great university that his parents pay for, with parents and a brother who love him, how is this guy so unappreciative that he gets kicked out of college and has to go to rehab?

Lucho went to school and studied to be an auto mechanic so that he could provide a better life for his family. What looked to me like poverty was a proud achievement for Lucho and his mother. They were proud to live together in their own house. Proud that Lucho had a good job and could pay the bills. Proud they could treat house guests to a wonderful meal. They had every right to be proud. They were happy. They had love. They had each other.

What was I proud of? Not a dang thing. I only had regrets. That needed to change. Instead of lamenting all that had happened, I wanted to be proud and satisfied like Lucho. As we got back to the garage, I came to a conclusion: If I did my best to be a good person, if I worked hard, treated people well, enjoyed life, and stayed humble, nothing else really mattered.

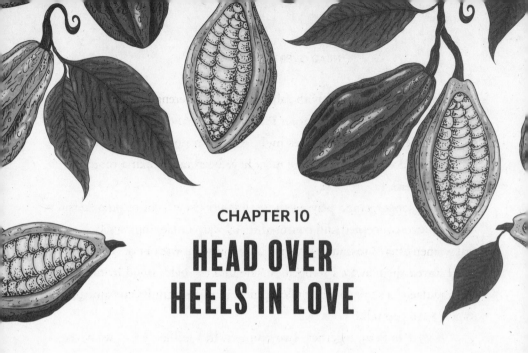

CHAPTER 10

HEAD OVER HEELS IN LOVE

After working hard all week, my first Saturday in Peru came around. I worked a half day on Saturday morning and came home in the afternoon wondering what folks in Cajamarca did on the weekend. Brian told me that Saturday night in Cajamarca was a time for getting drinks with friends and dancing. I was game but told Brian that I didn't want to drink. I hadn't had a drink in weeks, and I didn't want to fall back into old ways. Brian agreed to help me stay out of trouble.

Brian invited some friends who worked for FISAC and Automotriz Cajamarca to go out with us to a dancehall. When nightfall came, we piled into a taxi and drove to a field with a building planted in the middle.

Brian and the guys bought beers. I nursed a bottle of water as I took in the scene. The gang ingested their liquid courage and took off to dance with women. I'd only ever been in a place like this when I was drunk, and I wasn't sure if I knew how to have fun without alcohol.

The speakers pounded with salsas, cumbias, merengues, and Latino pop. The room was dark except for scattered bulbs and disco balls on the ceiling, which was several stories high. A bar ran down one of the long walls, flooded with people. There must have been more than a thousand people in there.

A tall, sober, gringo playing the wallflower drew a lot of onlookers. Most seemed concerned and confused that I wasn't enjoying myself. Several women offered to dance with me, but I figured it was out of sympathy, and I waved them away. I stepped outside into the field, stood by myself, and indulged in some lonely, philosophical moping until Brian came out to give me a pep talk.

We were in Peru, together. Two brothers. In a million years, we never could have guessed we'd end up there. But here we were, outside a dancehall, in a field under the stars. There was a party raging inside, and hundreds of women would love to dance with me. All I had to do was work up the courage to ask just one woman to dance, and I'd see how much fun it would be.

It was a compelling speech. I jumped up and down a few times and gave myself a good shaking to get rid of my nerves. I gave Brian a brotherly hug and started to head back in. Brian grabbed my arm and said something that would later prove clairvoyant.

"Bro, don't go falling in love with the first girl you dance with."

As I wandered around, several women made eye contact with me and smiled, but no one inspired me to make a move. Then I heard something above the pounding salsa music, the chatter, the stomping feet, and clinking beer bottles. It was a laugh. A loud, funny, authentic laugh. It cut through everything and drew me to it. I followed that laugh, and there she was with a big, beautiful smile. Her name was Nery. I asked her to dance the best I could, "Quieres bailar conmigo?" ("Do you want to dance with me?")

Nery was talking to a friend who gave her a why-not shrug. She grabbed my hand, and we walked out onto the dance floor. One song bled into the next, fast songs, slow songs, it all became a blur, a bending of time, hours collapsing into moments.

Falling in love is mysterious.

One moment, I was alone and free. The next moment, my life was all bound up with somebody else's—with Nery's.

At the end of the night, I asked Nery how I could see her again. She wrote down her phone number on a piece of paper. I told her I would call the next day, Sunday. She told me to call at 5:00 PM.

Then she took off an earring, gave it to me, and told me I'd better call. If not, she'd never get her earring back. I took the turquoise blue earring and put it in my pocket. I said, "Prometo." ("I promise.") I gave her a hug, and she went back to join her friends.

When 5:00 PM came around the next day, I was on the street with a pay phone in my hand. I dialed the number, and she answered. She gave me her address, but like a bonehead, I didn't have anything to write it down with.

I repeated the address over and over in my head as we wrapped up our conversation. I sprinted upstairs to our apartment and madly searched for paper and a pen while trying not to let that precious address slip away.

I finally found what I needed, jotted down the information, made a frantic dash downstairs, and waved for a taxi. I climbed in and stuck my paper in the driver's face. "Llevame aqui!" ("Take me here!"). He punched the gas, and we took off through Cajamarca.

We pulled up in front of the long, narrow, single-story building where Nery lived with a roommate. They shared a 150-square-foot room and slept in a bunk bed. They had a small bathroom. That was it.

Nery came out. My heart was racing. I gave her a big hug. I had doused myself in cologne for the occasion.

We started walking toward the Plaza de Armas, holding hands. I felt like a giant next to her. As we walked, we pieced together a conversation in Spanish, supplemented by a few English words she knew. I was already in love with her.

Nery worked at a hotel as a receptionist in the afternoons and got off at 10:00 PM. I asked how she got home, and she told me she walked. I asked if it was dangerous. She said it could be, but nothing scary had ever happened to her. I told her that I didn't like the idea of her being alone at night.

At the end of our first date, I asked Nery if I could start walking her home from work. She stopped, looked up at me, and said she would love that. I promised that while I was in town, she would never be in the dark streets alone.

Within a week of arriving in Peru, I had met a girl and fallen head over heels in love. We spent all our free time together. I worked during the day, ate lunch with her at midday, and after work, I explored Cajamarca and ate street food. At 10:00 PM I walked Nery home.

Before I knew it, three months had passed, and it was time for me to go home. I had mailed the rehab completion certificate to the university before leaving for Peru. Over the summer, I received notice from my dad that I'd been readmitted and could start school again in the fall.

Nery and I knew that our magical summer was coming to an end. We tried not to think about it. But as the days ticked off the calendar, we became more and more desperate, clinging to every single moment. But time stops for nobody. It will always slip from your grasp.

It rained the day we said goodbye. We had our final rendezvous on Nery's lunch break. After saying goodbye, I would head to the bus station to take the fifteen-hour bus ride back to Lima, and from there, I would fly home.

The moment before I turned and walked away, I remember looking at Nery standing in the rain. She was wearing a puffy white jacket she'd bought while I was in town. She had thought about that jacket for weeks before buying it. On her payday, we went together to the store to make the purchase. She'd worn it almost every day for the last two months. My heart was in my throat. God, I was going to miss seeing her in that jacket. Every ten feet or so, I looked back and waved. Tears streamed down her face. Eventually, I turned around, and she was no longer there.

During the weeks leading up to this day, we'd been planning our future together. I told Nery that I'd have another summer break in nine months. I asked her to wait for me until then. I promised to call her every day and come back in nine months. I told her that when I finished college, I would move down to Peru, work for the family business, and we'd get married. She promised to wait.

Nery's friends and family told her she was crazy and extremely naive to make such a promise or hold out any hope whatsoever for my return. These people didn't realize that the world I'd left behind wasn't all that hot for me. Being with Nery in Cajamarca was a much better version of life. Nery told the doubters that she had made a promise, and come what may, she would live up to it. If I didn't come back, that was my problem. But for her part, she would wait.

After three months, I announced to my family that I was dropping out of college and moving back down to Peru to get married. I couldn't live without Nery. I felt like my soul was shriveling and wasting away.

This news came as a big shock to my parents. But, alas, you don't get to choose your family and, lucky for me, mine are entrepreneurs— they believe in chasing dreams, not crushing them. In one of their finest moments, instead of squashing young love, they supported it.

There was one caveat. They wanted me to finish college. Instead of dropping out, they suggested a leave of absence. I jumped all over that and made plans to finish the current semester.

A month later I wrapped up school and flew back down to Peru. Nery didn't have to wait nine months. Only four.

On this second trip, I worked days as the financial administrator of our business with the mine and taught English at the local university in the evenings. My credentials for teaching English were that I spoke it and was in college. I wasn't much older than my students, but I did the best I could.

I rented a small apartment of my own, where Nery and I could spend time together. My two jobs provided just enough income to support myself on a shoestring budget. A few months after I came back, Nery and I got married, and she moved into the apartment with me. I was twenty-one years old. Nery was twenty-two.

We figured we shouldn't wait too long before getting married. Our plan was for Nery to come to the United States until I graduated. Then we would move back to Cajamarca so I could join the family business with the mine. What we didn't know was that by the time I graduated, there wouldn't be a mining business to come back to.

Immediately after tying the knot, we submitted paperwork to the US Consulate in Peru for a visa so that Nery could live and work legally in the United States. I had five months before my leave of absence was up and I had to return to school. We were sure this would be plenty of time for us to leave Peru together.

Five months came, and Nery didn't have a visa yet. I felt duty bound to honor my promise to my parents. Again, we had to say goodbye, this time as newlyweds. Again, I got on a bus alone and rode fifteen hours out of the mountains and down the coast.

It would be another ten months before Nery got her visa. I spent thousands of dollars on international calling cards. We spoke every day, and we waited. I flew down to Peru a couple of times, but the trips were too short. I had to get back to school. After ten brutal months of waiting, Nery received a parcel with her visa. We'd made it!

On the day Nery was scheduled to arrive in the United States, I drove to LAX to meet her. My brother had given me a beat-up old Honda Civic he no longer needed as he was now rarely in the States. I found out which escalator Nery would come down and plopped myself in a chair by it for what felt like an eternity. Then, there she was, descending the escalator and coming back into my life. We haven't been separated since.

CHAPTER 11

WHAT LIES BEYOND
THE MINE?

O n a typical workday for the next couple of years, Brian awoke at 4:30 AM and walked to a station where thousands of mine employees boarded chartered buses. The first fifty times Brian rode up to the mine, he looked out the window and marveled at the natural scenery, pondered the living situation of the campesinos, and reflected on the wild series of events that had brought him from San Diego, California, to the northern Peruvian Andes. During the fifty-first through five-hundredth ride, he slept on the bus just like everyone else.

The Minera Yanacocha maintenance department was an immense, multistory complex. There was a gigantic garage on the ground floor and administrative offices above. Inside the garage were twelve workstations for maintaining forty-foot-tall haulers. Imagine it—twelve machines, each the size of a three-story building, lined up side by side. The workstations were equipped with all the tools and diagnostic equipment needed to keep these massive work horses running right.

It was freezing cold most of the time. The normal temperature in the workshop was around 30 degrees Fahrenheit. When winds gusted through, which happened frequently, the temperature got down between 20 and 25 degrees.

There was always noise. Drilling. Sawing. Hammering. Metal tools being dropped on the floor. Workers talking and yelling. Music playing. Huge, powerful, engines being turned on and off. The smell of exhaust, gasoline, and lubricants filled the air.

Along the perimeter of the garage were small makeshift rooms where vendors sold parts. We had a room. Ferreyros had a room. There were about a dozen other vendors as well. When mechanics needed parts, they went into these rooms and took what they needed.

Our room had been custom built for us when our contract was signed. It was the smallest of the bunch. Ferreyros's room was built with the original construction of the structure, about twenty years before we showed up on the scene. Their room was more than five times the size of ours.

After getting his team going on the day's work, Brian headed up to the admin offices to make his rounds. It was mostly politics that determined how mechanics chose vendors for parts. The mechanics didn't choose their vendors. They followed instructions from higher-ups.

In a just and rational world, we should have been chosen every single time. Our prices were 30 to 40 percent cheaper across the board. The quality was a wash. In fact, we later proved that many of our parts were produced in the same factory in China as the Ferreyros parts. They were literally the exact same parts, except for the brand name stamped on them.

Given that we didn't have the resources or inclination to launch a Ferreyros-style graft campaign, Brian focused most of his attention on upper management. These folks were swayed more by the bottom line and career advancement than by gifts.

The major flaw in this strategy was that upper management turned over constantly. Just when we'd get an influential coalition together who would send word down to the mechanics to use our parts, somebody would get reassigned to another country, and our progress would recede. Little by little, workers started giving preference to Ferreyros again, and we'd have to start all over, working on the next batch of incoming managers.

In the admin office, Brian visited with contacts, arranged meetings, checked in, and reminded decision-makers who we were and how we could help them achieve their goals.

But that wasn't all Brian focused on in the admin offices. He had his eye on a very intriguing woman who worked there. Her name was Cecilia, known to most as "Ceci." Brian saw her at the gym most nights after work, and he managed to find a reason to swing by her desk often. After breaking up with his girlfriend, Brian was a free agent for the first time in a long time.

Over time, Brian and Cecilia developed a friendship and started going out for dinner together several nights a week. Cecilia was lovely, but very guarded. She had strong romantic feelings for Brian, but she was unwilling to give in to them.

She was a university graduate who had excelled in school and built an impressive career for herself at the mine. She wasn't interested in giving her life up to a man. The natural chain of events in Cajamarca would be for a woman to get married, have kids, and give up her career to stay home. That wasn't Cecilia. That wasn't the life she wanted. She felt she had to be careful, so she made Brian wait.

Brian took an active interest in ongoing conflicts between the mine and the local population. He attended a gigantic protest in the Plaza de Armas where thirty thousand people crowded into the town square. In a city of 120,000, this was an unbelievable turnout and spoke volumes about the intensity of the feelings.

A mix of campesinos and city dwellers stood together to oppose an extension of the mine into a part of the mountains called Cerro Quilish. *Cerro* means "mountain" and *Quilish* is an old Quechua word, Quechua being the native language spoken by the Incas before Spaniards showed up and colonized Peru.

Cerro Quilish was an important and beloved landmark, believed by many to have mystical powers. Unlike other mining sites, Cerro Quilish could be seen from the city.

Without public notice or attempting to secure public support in any way, Newmont worked with government officials behind the scenes to secure a mining claim to the land. They were proceeding with engineering plans to get the site ready for work. Cerro Quilish was estimated to hold 3.85 million ounces of gold. It was a very rich project.

However, the people of Cajamarca were not willing to have their magical mountain dug up and gutted. They were especially not ready to see it happening right in front of them, day in and day out, while going about their lives. Even though the law, the government, the money, and the power all appeared to be on the side of the mine, the people won the fight in the end.

Out in the mountains, campesinos made life a living hell for the mine. They blocked roads with boulders so employee caravans and supplies couldn't advance on the two-lane mountain highway. They cut power lines. They broke into the mine and destroyed machinery. They stole mining property that was left unattended. It was relentless, unending guerilla warfare out in the countryside.

Public pressure on any politician known to support the Cerro Quilish project, and the never-ending disruptions caused by the campesino community, became too much for Newmont to bear. They announced that they were abandoning the Cerro Quilish project permanently. The guerillas beat the gorilla. Brian was deeply impressed by the fortitude of the people and the public action that resulted. But he was also conflicted. Was he on the wrong side of this protest?

Brian decided that although he was doing business with the mine, he would do his best to show support for the people. When protests broke out, mine employees mostly stayed in their houses, commonly in gated communities, protected by security guards, in exclusive areas of the city.

But Brian didn't hide. He waded in. He attended protests. He listened to demands. He talked to people. He heard what they thought. He didn't hide the fact that he was a gringo who was in town doing business with the mine. His honesty and willingness to engage endeared him to protestors. They didn't attack Brian. They confided in him.

In the face of Newmont's ongoing conflict with the local community, and Ferreyros's increased attacks on our business, we could see what was destined to happen with our project.

In the beginning, we planned to get our operation at Minera Yanacocha running smoothly, and then we'd work this model at other mines. We planned to team up with more local businesses, import more products, and serve more mines.

But every mine we visited had a Ferreyros installation and the same problems in the community. As we neared the end of our three-year contract with the mine, the outlook for this business was not good.

It wasn't only business prospects that had us thinking about terminating our work with the mine. Brian was lonely and missed home. While he was out and about and busy, he was happy. But at night, alone in his apartment, a single, thirty-eight-year-old man in a foreign country with a business that was bound to fall apart, far from family, with no kids or prospects to have any, he ventured into some dark places in his mind.

Was he a failure? Was he destined to be alone the rest of his life? Was he going to have to be a bartender again?

CHAPTER 12

GOODBYE PERU?

At the end of 2005, as Brian and Dan were making final arrangements to exit our business with the mine, Brian attended a Newmont Christmas party in a little town called Baños del Inca, about twenty minutes outside of Cajamarca.

Amid the festivities, Brian saw Cecilia's best friend from the mine on the other side of the room. On several occasions, Cecilia and her friend had come to Brian's apartment to watch movies together. They had all gone out to eat as a group many times.

Brian jogged across the room and caught up with Cecilia's friend. He told her that he was done chasing Cecilia. He was leaving Cajamarca soon. It was over. He wished the friend and Cecilia all the best in the future, but he wouldn't be a part of it. Brian asked the friend to pass this information on. He gave the friend a hug. She kissed him on the cheek, as is the custom. Brian went back to the party, relieved. He was officially saying goodbye to this place.

Brian was sitting and watching the party unfold when Cecilia approached him. She asked if they could have a conversation in private, outside. Brian nodded and followed her out. They stood in front of the party hall in the cold air under a dark, star-filled sky. They looked at each other longingly. Neither could think of the right words to say. Words weren't what the situation called for. They kissed and decided to take a taxi home together.

That night led to more romantic interludes, but the timing was terrible. Brian was due to leave Cajamarca for good in a little over a month.

Right at the last minute, an interesting project surfaced. A friend of a friend introduced Brian and Dan to a gentleman who was building an industrial trout farm in the city of Huanuco. Huanuco is another mountain town, far south of Cajamarca at a lower altitude, around six thousand feet. The fish would be sent to Lima for export.

Brian had mixed feelings about doing another project. He was yearning for home, but the development with Cecilia acted as a counterbalance. If the project details checked out, he'd stay and pursue the budding romance a little longer and find out if it was the real thing.

Brian went to scout the trout operation and was convinced of its viability. The leader of the project appeared hardworking and trustworthy. The fundamentals made sense. They'd farm trout in the mountains, flash freeze them, and then it was almost a straight line to the coast for export.

Dan spoke to everybody he knew about the new concept and was introduced to a fish importer in China who expressed serious interest in being a buyer. Just like that, something brand new was lining up. Brian moved to Lima to put it together.

While in Lima, Brian and Ceci talked on the phone daily and saw each other frequently. Brian made short trips back to Cajamarca, and Ceci came to Lima when her schedule permitted.

For five months, the new venture seemed to be clicking right along. Dan lined up buyers for fish in China, and Brian put everything together to manage logistics and deliver a high-quality product.

Then, without warning, the project owner in Huanuco disappeared. Brian called and called, but there was no answer. When Brian went to Huanuco, nobody could say where the guy had gone. It was a mystery.

This was a gut punch. With no business to work on and therefore no prospects for future income, Brian was forced to decide. Did he want to move back to Cajamarca, pursue Cecilia, and try to get a job with the mine? Or did he want to go home to San Diego and regroup?

After several heartfelt and tearful conversations with Cecilia, Brian made his decision. He needed to go home and figure out what to do next. Without a business to work on, what future could there possibly be in Peru?

CHAPTER 13

NOW WHAT?

In the United States, Brian moved in with our mom. A week earlier he was a successful American businessman working on a deal to buy frozen trout in Peru and sell it to fish importers in China. He was dating a beautiful Peruvian woman. Six months earlier, he was the boss of a multimillion-dollar business selling equipment to the world's biggest gold mine. He was earning good money and he was known and respected in town as the unique gringo who cared about the locals.

Back home, he was still the same person, but circumstances had changed. He carried all the memories and experiences from Peru with him, but it was hard to get over the fact that he was living in a small upstairs loft in a two-bedroom townhouse, sharing a bathroom with his mother. I remember one time overhearing Brian and my mom bicker over whose turn it was to shower.

Despite the weirdness of the situation, the break did Brian a lot of good. In Cajamarca, he had never been able to really process and get over his previous, eleven-year relationship. He was always working too hard and staying too busy.

He hadn't come to terms with having gone from being a young man in his midtwenties to what felt like the doorway of middle age with this one woman, and in the end, what did he have to show for it? No kids. No marriage. No nothing.

Brian coped by getting in the best shape of his life. He worked out hard daily. He ate healthy. He spent time with old friends, played basketball on Saturday mornings, slept well, played Scrabble, talked for hours on end with our mom, and watched movies at night.

During this same period, Dan had some major soul-searching to do. He was sixty-six years old, and another one of his businesses had just flamed out. On the other hand, unlike his other ventures, he had exited the mining business voluntarily with a good nest egg. Miraculously, he had reconnected with and married Nancy, the love he'd lost forty-five years ago as a young naval officer. Peru and marriage had cured most of my bad behavior. These were big wins.

Still, seeing another business shut down was disappointing. When, for the love of God, would he start an enduring business? Was he destined to spend his entire life starting over?

The more he thought about it, the more determined he became. He'd keep starting over until the day he died, if called to do so. This was the life he had chosen. The life he knew how to live. He was an adventurer. An entrepreneur. A riverboat gambler. It was too late to change now.

Most sixty-six-year-old men would have been thinking about how to use their money for retirement. Dan was looking for a table to belly up to and a hand to play. To his mind, the money in the bank was earmarked for one thing only: getting a new business up and running.

As for me, I was a young married man trying to support myself and my wife, and now that there was no family business waiting for me in Peru, reality came crashing in. When I graduated from college, I would have to get a real job. I ended up working at the least entrepreneurial job imaginable: I did payroll for the Department of Defense.

Nery took a job bagging groceries at a local supermarket. Her English was so limited that she couldn't do much else in the beginning. Over time, she worked her way up to being a cashier at Target. Then she went on to be the state's top bra saleswoman at Macy's. Finally, she settled in as a teller working for UnionBank before making the decision to be a stay-at-home mom after we had kids.

Our life was good, even though I was miserable at work. Also, Nery was expecting to move back to Cajamarca after I finished school. She couldn't have known at the time that she'd never move back to Peru. She's been living in the United States for twenty years now.

CHAPTER 14

PERU REDUX

Dan was 100 percent committed to pursuing a business with Brian, come what may. Brian reached the same conclusion. He wasn't interested in working for anybody else. There was only one way forward: they had to take their money and invest it in something. The most important thing was that they stick together.

Dan and Brian thought and debated, thrashed and envisioned, and ultimately came to the same conclusion: their only real competitive advantage was in Peru. Brian spoke the language and understood the culture. They had many business contacts in positions to help. It was cheap to live in Peru, which would make their capital last longer. Yes, Peru felt right.

They thought about what they'd seen over the last several years. What and where were underutilized resources that could be made productive? Brian's mind kept landing on those vast stretches of barren wasteland on the northern Peruvian coast that flourished and sprang to life when infrequent rains finally showered upon them.

Could something grow there? Yes, something could grow, if there was water. But there wasn't any water. That's why most of the land was uncultivated. Only coastal land situated on a river, or downstream from dams or irrigation projects, could be farmed.

Did any of the uncultivated land have groundwater? Could wells be drilled and water pumped up to irrigate the land?

At our mom's dining room table, Brian started researching. Yes, indeed, a lot of northern Peruvian coastal land had groundwater. But nobody had found a way to use it profitably, and it remained untapped.

I was sitting with Brian one evening watching George W. Bush give his State of the Union address. Bush mentioned a policy to encourage the mixing of ethanol into gasoline to reduce the nation's dependence on fossil fuels.

Brian and I had a good chuckle when, right after Bush's mention of the policy, the camera panned over to senators and congressmen from Iowa yucking it up, high-fiving, smiling, and shaking hands.

The corn lobby was getting a big boost. Corn was the number one source of ethanol in the United States. Shortly thereafter, a law was passed giving refineries a big tax credit for blending refined gas with ethanol.

As Brian researched, something dawned on him. Sugar cane is a far more efficient raw material than corn for producing ethanol. Using sugar cane for ethanol would make the ethanol much cheaper.

Could some of that barren coastal land with groundwater be used to grow sugar cane for producing ethanol?

Would the tax credit still apply if ethanol was imported from Peru?

Could an ethanol producer in Peru make a profit, considering the capital investment in groundwater and machinery?

Brian researched and pondered and ran the numbers over and over again. The answer to all these questions appeared to be yes.

Back at our mother's dining room table, Brian showed his findings to Dan. Dan agreed that the numbers and concept made sense. They decided to go for it.

Dan would line up investors. This project would require a lot of funding. Brian would head back down to Peru to put on a dog-and-pony show along the northern Peruvian coast to get buy-in from whoever owned the desert. He'd also meticulously compile a list of all the necessary resources, land, machines, people, and logistics needed to produce exportable ethanol.

Finally, the moment arrived. Mom drove Brian to the airport. He was ready to transition back from a thirty-eight-year-old unemployed man living with his mother to a mysterious, dignified, jet-setting, international entrepreneur.

CHAPTER 15

THE ETHANOL DREAM

Brian knew that desert communities would be starving for economic development. With no source of running water for agriculture, these communities were destined for suffocating poverty without much hope of things getting better. His concept could do a lot of good for these people.

Given that finding land with the right kind of water was critical, Brian wanted to network with someone at the National Water Authority. A longtime friend from the mine had a cousin at the agency.

Officials at the water authority were kind enough to put Brian in touch with a consultant who helped small villages in northern Peru find development projects. This consultant lined up meetings for Brian to present his plans to landowners.

Since the 1960s, a lot of land in Peru is owned by *comunidades campesinas*, campesino communities. Due to centuries of Spanish imperialism, most of the wealth in Peru up until the 1960s had been held by a few dozen families with lineage back to Spanish conquistadores and courtesans.

In 1968, Juan Velasco Alvarado, a Peruvian general, overthrew the government and installed a left-leaning, military dictatorship. One of his key reforms was breaking up the haciendas, vast land tracts owned by Peru's rich elite.

The government redistributed land to newly formed cooperatives in campesino communities with boards of directors democratically elected by the people. The board of directors makes decisions about how to use the redistributed land.

To push his project through, Brian would need to win over the hearts and minds of the community board members who controlled the northern coastal desert.

Brian's target locations were extremely remote little towns on the edges of huge deserts that produced virtually nothing and where it never rained.

The people farmed and survived off small-scale wells and an occasional puny creek. They scratched out a meager living in small, sandy communities, working day in and day out under an unrelenting, unforgiving sun.

One by one, Brian visited these small towns where no foreigner had ever set foot. Some were right next to the Pan-Americana Highway. Others required turning onto a narrow road and driving several miles deeper into the desert's interior until Brian and the consultant came to a small gathering of houses.

Out in the desert villages, Brian was treated as an honored guest. In simple, gray brick rooms with concrete floors and roofs made of bunched-up hay or large dried leaves, sitting around sturdy wooden tables in wooden chairs, Brian gave his presentation to campesino community board members.

The board members were generally dressed in weathered jeans, leather sandals, and button-down long-sleeved shirts with the sleeves rolled up. When they worked out in the sun for long stretches, they rolled the sleeves down to protect their skin. They wore straw hats typical of the region. Their faces were dark brown and wrinkled from the sun.

Sweating from the heat, Brian laid out the facts in perfect Spanish. He explained the tax credit for ethanol in the United States. He pointed out that the land was fertile when it rained, that there was extensive groundwater underneath the ground controlled by the community, and that sugar cane could grow extremely well in their soil.

Finally came the clincher. Brian explained that the communities controlled enough land to produce tens or hundreds of millions of dollars' worth of ethanol per year. Brian stated that he and his partner Dan would raise all the investment funding and manage the project. All the community had to do was agree to permit use of the land. In exchange for that, they'd receive a percentage of the revenue.

After presentations, board members gave Brian tours of their little towns, generally consisting of between twenty and fifty houses.

Brian looked at the sunbaked concrete houses with skinny chickens and skinny goats who survived off corn and desert weeds, moseying around in the yards. He saw small wells dug on every property. These wells watered humble gardens that provided the means of living for the townspeople.

He saw children playing soccer on rugged, rocky, dirt fields. Brian looked out from the villages at the endless vistas of potentially productive land that lay unused. You could walk right out into it from the villages, and if you did so, you could keep walking forever across the dry, empty terrain.

When the tour was complete, Brian was always invited for lunch. The lunches were usually a simple thin soup, stewed meat with a heaping mound of white rice, and fruit juice. The meals were delicious and made with a lot of love.

Almost unbelievably, after a couple dozen trips to the desert, six campesino communities signed memos of understanding. The memos said that if Brian and Dan could raise the necessary funding to buy equipment, pump groundwater, grow sugar cane on a large scale, and convert it into ethanol, they could use the land and the water underneath in return for a percentage of the revenues from the sale of ethanol.

With rights secured to enough land to produce hundreds of millions of dollars' worth of ethanol per year, Brian started working on refining the rest of his numbers. He started pricing equipment, logistics, and infrastructure. He plugged in revenue numbers. He plugged in labor costs. As he filled in more and more numbers, his dreams and expectations grew. This looked like a big-time, highly lucrative project.

Brian sent the numbers to Dan, and Dan started making the rounds of investment bankers and investors. There was immediate and serious interest. Soon Dan had several parties in a bidding war to fund the deal.

After six months back in Peru, Brian was feeling extremely positive, so much so that he started dreaming of what it would be like to become a millionaire. After all, if this project were to come off as he imagined, he would undoubtedly become one many times over. Not only that, but he could transform the lives of thousands of people living in humble shacks out in the desert, create a ton of jobs, and do meaningful charitable work.

CHAPTER 16

WHEN ONE DOOR CLOSES...

It wasn't just business that was lifting Brian up. As soon as he was back in Peru, he called Ceci to say he was in the country. He asked if she'd like to come visit him, and she said yes. When they saw each other, there was an explosion of passion. They'd missed each other much more than they'd realized.

Ceci joined Brian as he traveled around from city to city. When Brian could, he took trips to Cajamarca. They went together to the beach and to the big outdoor markets. They took nature walks in the mountains surrounding Cajamarca. They watched movies and went out to dinners. They took road trips up the coast to the beautiful beaches in Peru's northernmost department, Tumbes, where they stayed in romantic cottages ten feet from the sand. They were falling in love.

Neither Ceci nor Brian were interested in settling into a traditional family structure. Ceci was on a fast upward trajectory with the mine. It looked like she'd be one of the few Cajamarcans to get promoted into management with Newmont. She'd have the opportunity to travel to mines all over the world. This was her dream. She wanted to build a career, make good money, and travel to other countries.

Brian was on board with Ceci's life plan. Brian was an adventurer. At age thirty-eight, with no kids, and a big entrepreneurial project to get up and running, he wasn't looking to settle down. The way he saw it, if Ceci was sent to other mines in other parts of the world, he'd go with her. He had come to accept that maybe he was meant to be a free spirit for the rest of his life, a rambler, with no kids and no wife.

As Brian approached his eighth month back in Peru, everything looked to be as good as it could possibly be. He was in love. He was living cheaply. His project was coming along. He felt challenged and fulfilled.

As part of his work, Brian monitored news about the ethanol industry. One morning, a very alarming article showed up in his inbox. The article said that the tax credit he'd based the entire project on was in danger of being revoked.

The tax credit was put in place for environmental reasons and as a subsidy to the corn industry in the United States. However, there were unintended consequences. People like Brian were working on projects to use sugar cane from other countries to produce ethanol, and their prices were going to undercut US-produced, corn-based ethanol. The administration wanted to keep this from happening.

This article freaked Brian out to his core. He opened his projections and adjusted the numbers to see how they'd look without the tax credit. When he changed the numbers, everything turned red. He choked with fear.

Brian called Dan to make him aware of the situation, and Dan said he would start investigating the matter right away. Brian made a snap decision to get on a bus to Lima, where he could visit the US embassy and get more information. While Brian was in Lima, the tax credit was officially overturned. Just like that, his big project was up in smoke.

Brian sat in a hotel room in Lima trying to figure out what to do next. His heart was broken. He thought about the six campesino communities he would have to visit and give the bad news. It would probably make those communities never want to work with another outsider ever again.

He'd been drawing a monthly salary from the company's savings. He was living affordably in Peru, so he hadn't made a very big dent in the company's capital. However, he was taking that money as compensation for putting a new business together. If he wasn't doing that, was it right for him to keep drawing a salary? Would Dan agree to keep funding his living expenses until they found something new?

Brian also worried about what Ceci would think. When she'd met him and started falling for him, he was managing a successful business. Over the last several months, she had been falling for him in the context of his big, new exciting business. Now he would have to tell her he'd failed at pulling off the new venture.

For the next couple of days, Brian wandered around in a terrible, gloomy funk. He couldn't figure out the right path forward. The thoughts cycling through his mind were driving him crazy. Finally, he decided to sit down and make a list of all the things that he and Dan might be able to get into. He typed out every opportunity that he'd heard about or seen since he got back to Peru. Putting new ideas down in writing gave Brian a moment of hope.

After typing up the list, Brian decided to lay down on his hotel bed and watch TV for a while. He wanted to let his mind relax. As soon as his head hit the pillow and his thumb pushed the power button on the remote, his flip phone started to buzz.

It was Ceci. She said hello in a deadly serious tone. Brian asked what was wrong. There was an unnaturally long pause. Fighting back tears, Ceci told Brian that she was pregnant. She'd thought it through, and she wanted to have the baby. She and Brian were going to be parents.

Brian's field of vision went white, and his body went numb. He hadn't realized it until that very moment, but the idea of being a father was terrifying to him. He heard Ceci talking on the phone, but her voice now sounded like it was a million miles away, barely coming through a shroud of buzzing white noise that was clouding Brian's ears. Brian did his best to be present, and he managed to mumble through the rest of the conversation. None of this was reassuring to Ceci, but there was nothing more that Brian could give. His system was in shock.

Brian said goodbye, closed the phone, left the room, and went for a walk around Lima.

CHAPTER 17

HELLO CACAO

Brian decided to propose marriage to Ceci. He loved her and probably would have asked her to marry him eventually. The pregnancy just speeded things up a bit. He packed his belongings and took the fifteen-hour bus ride from Lima to Cajamarca. Ceci accepted Brian's proposal.

Ceci and Brian rented a small apartment. Ceci continued working at the mine during her pregnancy. Brian began giving private English lessons to mine employees. For managers who wanted to leave Cajamarca someday, a certification for English as a second language was a big plus.

During every moment of free time, Brian networked, looking for the next deal. It had been five years since Brian and Dan had first set foot in Cajamarca. After five years of effort, Brian now found himself teaching English to make ends meet. Yet that pesky entrepreneurial dream was still there.

Ceci's brother-in-law, Beto, was friends with the local manager of Sodexho, the huge French company that operated the cafeteria at Minera

Yanacocha. They were looking for local suppliers of certain fruits and vegetables, primarily bananas, for the mine. Beto let the manager know that
his new brother-in-law, Brian, was an expert at in-country logistics and
was looking to start a new business. This piqued the manager's interest,
and he asked Beto to arrange a meeting.

Brian learned that Sodexho was making a push to source as many
of the mine's cafeteria items as possible from within the Department of
Cajamarca, of which Cajamarca city is the capital.

This was challenging because most of Cajamarca's territory is at a high
altitude, in the Andes, where agriculture is sparse. There was, however, a
remote region in the very northeastern corner of the department that had
extremely productive agricultural land. The two principal cities in that
zone are Jaén and San Ignacio.

Sodexho had not been able to find anyone willing to go back and
forth between Cajamarca and either Jaén or San Ignacio to buy produce
and ship it to the mine. The principal reason for this was that no one
in Cajamarca wanted to go down the eastside of the mountains into
the jungle.

For many months, Brian had consistently attended chamber of commerce
meetings in Cajamarca, hoping to come across an opportunity. One of the
meetings he attended in late 2007 focused on exporting.

This topic was near and dear to Brian's heart. He'd done a lot of
research over the previous year on how to get Peruvian goods out of the
country. At this particular meeting, several exportable Peruvian products
were discussed by presenters, including cacao.

When the meeting was over, none of the other attendees showed any
interest whatsoever in cacao. The presenter who talked about cacao stood
all alone, while the others had crowds around them. Brian approached
him and asked how he could learn more.

The presenter gave Brian the name of his boss, the director of agricultural development for the Department of Cajamarca. Brian tracked down the director to set up a meeting.

When Brian told the director of agriculture that he wanted to know more about cacao, the director all but scoffed in Brian's face. Why did he want to know about cacao? It was such a boring idea. There was no growth in it.

Plus, working with cacao would mean going to Jaén, and surely, no self-respecting gringo with contacts at the mine would want to head out to that backwater. Brian was confused as to why the director had sent somebody to the chamber of commerce meeting if cacao was such an odious product. It turned out to be an act of bureaucratic grandstanding. The government wanted to appear equitable. In private, the director expressed his true feelings.

The fact that the director was so strongly against cacao made it even more intriguing to Brian. He insisted on knowing more. Brian told the director he had a contact at Sodexho, and he could investigate buying products for the mine's cafeteria if he were to take a trip to Jaén.

Finally, the director relented and promised to give Brian an email introduction to Sarah Paredes, the government worker in charge of promoting cacao in Jaén.

When Brian told friends and acquaintances that he was making plans to go to Jaén on business, they thought he was nuts. Was he looking to be kidnapped? Beyond agriculture, Jaén had a reputation for organized crime.

All the pushback only served to whet Brian's appetite. If everyone was so dead set against this opportunity, it meant no one was paying attention to it. He might be able to find something that was being overlooked.

Brian wanted to get Dan involved from the very start. He wanted a second pair of eyes on this project every step of the way to make sure they didn't have any blind spots. Dan made plans to fly to Cajamarca for the first time since they'd exited the mining business almost a year and a half earlier.

When Dan showed up in Cajamarca, he and Brian embraced. More than any time in the past, Brian and Dan felt like true partners. When two people go through hard times together and manage to survive, their bond grows stronger. This was the case with Brian and Dan.

Not only had Dan helped to raise Brian starting from age eleven, they'd been hustling together for the last five years as teammates. They'd shared victories. They'd been through the wringer together. Yet there they were, united, ready to go on their next voyage. They felt strong, excited, and optimistic.

CHAPTER 18
JAÉN

I t was May 2008 when Dan arrived in Cajamarca. Brian's first child, a daughter named Amara, had just been born. Dan held the baby and met Ceci's family. After a couple of days, the two adventurers went to the bus station early one morning and boarded a bus to Chiclayo. As they rode up and out of Cajamarca, they looked out at the never-ending mountains they'd come to know so well. The campesinos out working the land were now a regular part of their lives.

Seventeen hours after leaving Cajamarca, the duo arrived in Jaén. The first word that popped into Brian's mind when he saw Jaén was *chaos*. Streams of motorcycles buzzed by with two or three people aboard. Freight trucks clogged the streets, honking and maneuvering. Moto taxis were everywhere.

When Dan and Brian climbed off the bus, a second word came instantly to mind: *heat*. Jaén is one of the hottest places in all Peru.

As they grabbed their bags and walked out onto the street, a third word came to mind: *foreigners*. People immediately gawked and did double takes. The two gringos were a major curiosity.

Dan and Brian took a taxi to the hotel Sarah Paredes had booked for them. Before going in, Brian marveled at the streets teeming with movement. There was a row of restaurants and a casino on the hotel side of the street and a long array of shops on the other. The sidewalks were packed with people. The traffic was frenzied.

To the north and east, Brian saw lush, rolling jungle. The ridges and peaks were covered in vegetation. To the south and west, where they had entered the city, he could see huge mountains that reminded him of the city of Cajamarca.

At 7:30 PM, Dan and Brian met Sarah in the restaurant she chose, next to the Plaza de Armas. When Sarah arrived, Brian and Dan were already seated and easy to find. Look for a couple of gringos and that was them.

Sarah introduced herself and sat down. She explained that her role with the government was to promote exports from this part of Cajamarca. While she was tasked with promoting all exports, there was currently a special push to sell more cacao at higher prices, and Sarah was leading the charge.

At that time in the chocolate industry, there was a burgeoning scene of chocolate makers focusing on fine-flavored chocolate. Instead of following the traditional path of treating chocolate as a candy, a mere vehicle for delivering sugar and other flavorings, these chocolate makers were starting to treat chocolate as a complex, sophisticated creation in its own right.

A realization was dawning on some in the industry that cacao is not a homogeneous ingredient. Like wine grapes, the flavor of cacao varies from variety to variety and place to place. Genetics, terroir, and post-harvest processing matter and can be leveraged to produce a wide range of extraordinary flavors.

Sarah was aware of this market trend, and so were Dan and Brian. They had both done research on the industry prior to making the trip. Sarah wanted these gringos to help her find out whether the cacao growing around Jaén could be considered fine flavored. And if so, what would need to happen to start selling cacao at a premium price into that market?

Dan and Brian let Sarah know that while they were in town, they needed to do some legwork on potentially sourcing fruits and vegetables for Sodexho. They appreciated her laser focus on cacao, but they'd also need to look at other types of farms.

Sarah told them not to worry. Most of the farms in the region were small hold, multicrop, agroforestry-type farms with many crops growing side by side on a single plot of land. This was not a zone of big, single-crop plantations. There would be plenty of opportunities for them to see everything they needed to see.

After dinner, at 9:30 PM on a weekday, it felt like a block party was underway in the Plaza de Armas. The air was filled with music turned up full blast—a mix of salsa, cumbia, afro-Peruvian beats, and reggaeton. Dozens of moto taxis were at the curbs, and each driver was a DJ unto himself. All the bars blasted their own playlists. Add to that the clamor of motorcycles zipping around the city and a thousand or more residents laughing and chattering. It was loud.

It was still hot out. Women, young and old alike, strutted around in short shorts, sandals, and thin, revealing shirts. Young men had their shirts off, and gathered in groups, eyeing the girls.

Every bench in the Plaza de Armas was occupied by laughing, chatty families and friends. Food carts were out to service the evening crowd.

Dan and Brian considered wading in, but they'd just shown up and appeared to be the only gringos in town. Best not to make a spectacle on their first night. They walked with Sarah through the bustling nightlife back to their hotel and called it a day.

CHAPTER 19

TASTING THE DREAM

Bright and early the next day, Dan and Brian met Sarah in front of the hotel. With sweat already running down their faces, they piled into a pickup truck with a hired driver. Although the revelry on the plaza had lasted well past midnight, at 7:00 AM everyone appeared to be back on the street, hard at work. Did the pulse of Jaén ever slow down?

Driving east out of Jaén, you quickly see rich agricultural land with fruit trees of all sorts—mangos, coconuts, bananas, *maracuya* (passionfruit), other native fruits, cacao trees, sugar cane, and coffee. You see wide, flat rice farms.

In the middle of this impressive display of Mother Earth's productive power, you see humans. They appear small and delicate, working in the enormity of the countryside with machetes, tractors pulled by beasts of burden, and wheelbarrows, collecting their harvest.

Sarah motioned the driver to turn onto a small dirt road. She waved a badge at a security guard who pulled open a gate for the truck to drive through.

Dan and Brian got out, stretched, and looked around. They had arrived at a government owned and operated germplasm bank that was housed on an expansive farm filled with groves of trees organized by species. This would be their first look at agricultural products in the region.

Dan and Brian walked around the farm looking at plants and trees, while listening to commentary from Sarah. It became clear in short order that sourcing fruits and vegetables for Sodexho was a nonstarter.

Fruits and vegetables were not cash crops in the zone. The infrastructure did not exist to harvest and export these items on a large scale. It would be hard to find farm partners growing enough to make a project based on those crops viable. Given this realization while at the germplasm bank, Dan and Brian turned all their energy on learning what they could about cacao.

One section of the farm was dedicated entirely to cacao, and alongside the cacao trees was a sample postharvest processing station. Dan and Brian had read a bit about cacao postharvest processing, and they were very interested to see it done with their own eyes.

Cacao needs to be fermented in order to taste like chocolate. Inside a cacao pod, which looks like an American football with a husk as thick and hard as a squash, there are roughly 30–40 seeds. The seeds are the size of a big grape, and inside the pod they are surrounded by a sweet white gel called mucilage.

To get the seeds out of the cacao pod, you need to break the pod open on a rock—or, more commonly, hack it open with a machete—and scoop the seeds out.

Sarah asked one of the farm employees to hack open some pods so Dan and Brian could suck on the seeds. The farm worker complied and handed Dan and Brian each his own open cacao pod.

Dan and Brian grabbed the seeds with their fingers and popped them in their mouths. The slimy mucilage left a sticky, wet residue on their hands. Sarah instructed them to just suck the gel off the outside and not bite into the seed. Unfermented cacao is very bitter.

The mucilage was sweet and citrusy, like lemonade nectar. After they sucked the sweet goo off the outside of the seeds, Sarah told Dan and Brian to spit the seeds onto the farm floor.

Sarah explained that the gel is what causes cacao to ferment. When cacao pods are cut open, yeast spores from the air fall onto the mucilage. To ferment cacao, you put wet seeds into a wooden box (or some other receptacle) and cover it with banana leaves, a burlap sack, or a plank of wood.

When you limit exposure to oxygen, yeast starts to eat the sugar, and this kicks off fermentation. After fermenting for 5–7 days, cacao beans turn from white to brown and start to smell and taste like chocolate.

Sarah called Dan and Brian over to look at a fermentation box. She took the top off, and the smell of vinegar came wafting out. Amazingly, though, somewhere in that vinegar aroma was a faint hint of chocolate.

When fermentation is complete, cacao is laid out to dry under the sun. The government facility was drying cacao on the ground, just like everybody else in the region. Workers put recently fermented cacao on top of black, woven polyurethane tarps that were spread out on the farm floor.

After 3–5 days drying in the sun, a brittle shell forms. The dried cacao is then loaded into sacks for export. This is the base ingredient for all chocolate. The quality of the fermentation and drying processes, along with the genetics of the bean, are key factors in determining how good the chocolate will taste.

On a white piece of cloth on the ground, there were six cacao pods of different sizes, shapes, textures, and colors ranging from deep, bright red to purple, green, orange, and yellow. Some of the pods were long and slender. Others were stocky and wide. Some had little bumps all over the outside. Some had shallow or deep ridges.

The bright red and purple pods were industrial, high-yield, disease-resistant hybrids that were being planted more and more. They were easy to maintain and produced high volumes of cacao for farmers to sell.

However, almost everyone recognized that these cacaos don't make very good-tasting chocolate. Sarah expressed her concern that if farmers continued to plant these industrial hybrids, they would be doomed forever to receive rock-bottom prices for their crops.

After discussing the industrial hybrids, Sarah pointed to the yellow, green, and orange pods. She explained that these cacaos were native to the zone. The trees were less productive, but the cacao made better chocolate.

In fact, you could taste the difference in the mucilage. Brian and Dan had been sucking seeds out of a bright, red industrial pod and enjoying it. Sarah motioned to an employee to cut open a yellow pod for them to taste. They were shocked at how much more intense and delicious the flavors were. Their business instincts ignited, and they looked at each other knowingly. Here was an opportunity.

They spent the next day in a building belonging to the National University of Cajamarca. Brian, Dan, and Sarah planned to be there from early morning until late in the day. Presidents of associations from the local cacao-growing towns would be there presenting and networking.

After thirty minutes of small talk and mingling, the meeting got underway. President after president got up to state his point of view.

When lunchtime came around, the attendees formed a line to meet the gringos who were interested in cacao. To a man, every single person invited Dan and Brian to take a tour of his village.

Brian collected contact information and let people know that they were leaving town in two days, but they'd be back soon. At the end of the procession, an individual with a particularly intense presence stepped forward.

He walked up close to Brian, stuck out his hand for a handshake, and looked Brian searchingly in the eyes for several seconds. Just when Brian was starting to feel uncomfortable, the gentleman flashed a charming smile.

The fellow introduced himself as Noé Vasquez, president of the cacao growers' association of the district of Huarango. Noé told Brian

and Dan that they absolutely must come to Huarango if they were interested in cacao.

Noé was average height for a Peruvian. He had thick black hair,
chubby jowls, a sturdy, stocky body, and the most inquisitive black eyes.
Dan and Brian were struck by his obvious intelligence and dignified cha-
risma. They found themselves drawn to him and were won over by his
willingness to express his ambitions. Noé mentioned right there, in that
first encounter, that the district of Huarango wanted a project that would
improve their situation. If Dan and Brian would come visit, the entire
district would roll out the red carpet.

It wasn't just that. Noé paused for a moment, then leaned in close to
look at Brian and Dan with a serious expression. When Noé was sure he
had their attention, he said in almost a whisper, "We have special cacao in
Huarango." There was a faint smile on his lips now. He squinted his eyes
and tilted his head back, allowing what he had said to sink in.

Brian told Noé that he and Dan would be back soon and would defi-
nitely visit the district of Huarango. Noé handed over a business card with
his information, they shook hands, and Noé walked away.

On their third and final day in town, Brian and Dan found themselves
on the street early in the morning waiting for Sarah. The heat was already
bearing down, the noise and motion of the city already at a fever pitch.

When Sarah arrived, they headed east out of Jaén on the same route
they'd taken to visit the germplasm bank. After forty-five minutes, the
truck turned onto a bumpy dirt road, and two farm dogs started snarling
and barking hysterically.

The driver parked the truck near a simple farmhouse constructed from
uneven eucalyptus planks. The dogs continued threatening until Don
Fernando Ruiz, the farm's owner, showed up smiling and called them off.

Don Fernando was barefoot. He had on brown pants rolled up to his
knees, a shirt with a dirty collar, and a worn-out baseball cap. When he

smiled, his teeth shone white, in stark contrast to his bronzed, dark brown skin. His thick black salt-and-pepper hair stuck out from beneath his cap.

Don Fernando motioned to the group to follow him into the farmhouse.

Inside, Don Fernando invited everyone to sit down at a simple wooden table with plates, forks, teacups, and two plates filled with bread and small bananas. Don Fernando's wife came in to ask the group if they'd prefer tea or coffee with their breakfasts. Even though it was excruciatingly hot, everyone took coffee, and thanked their lovely hostess for her hospitality.

After serving hot water and putting tins of instant coffee and sugar on the table with serving spoons, Don Fernando's wife sat down, and everyone ate bread and bananas, drank coffee, and chatted.

Both Don Fernando and his wife were barefoot. The dining room had a dirt floor, and the eucalyptus walls were bare except for two framed pictures, one of a fair-skinned, blonde, blue-eyed Jesus and the second of the Virgin Mary, cradling baby Jesus in her arms.

The door was open, and all kinds of animals squawked just outside. Occasionally, a critter approached the open doorway, only to be shooed away aggressively by Don Fernando's wife.

From the open doorway, Brian had a beautiful view of the farm. Some of the plants were tall, reaching high into the jungle sky, their wide, thin leaves soaking up all the sunlight they could to manifest sweet, juicy, bulbous tropical fruits.

Closer to the farm floor, Brian saw coffee bushes with their small, bright red cherries that looked like mistletoe. In between the short coffee bushes and the tall fruit trees, Brian saw cacao.

The farm floor was covered with fallen, decomposing leaves, rotting cacao pods, and a plethora of other organic, compostable material. No compost bin needed. The entire farm floor was composting.

After breakfast, Don Fernando led the group on a tour of his farm. Brian and Dan noticed that cacao trees and banana trees were almost always growing side by side, and asked Don Fernando why.

Don Fernando explained that cacao trees don't like a lot of sun. Banana trees, with their long, light green, drooping leaves that fall on either side of their thick stems, provide just the right amount of shade for the cacao trees below.

Don Fernando led them to a fermentation and drying station he had set up. Like the germplasm bank, Don Fernando had a wooden box for fermenting cacao. He also had a raised drying table, with a plastic tarp to protect drying cacao from the rain.

The box and dryer table were completely empty and clean, as if they hadn't been used in a long while. Brian asked Don Fernando why.

Don Fernando told Dan, Brian, and Sarah to follow him over to a cacao grove and he would give them the answer. In the middle of the grove, Don Fernando pointed to a plastic tarp on the farm floor under a gap in the trees where the sun could shine through. The tarp was covered in drying cacao.

A collection of animals had followed the humans into the grove, and they all took an interest in the drying cacao. Dogs came over and sniffed it. Chickens pecked at it. A duck walked onto the tarp and dragged its backside over it.

Brian asked if they should shoo the animals away. Don Fernando shook his head no. It didn't matter; they'd just come back. Brian got closer to the drying cacao and, as he looked down at the tarp, saw ants, beetles, and worms crawling around.

Don Fernando pointed to thick, black nylon bags leaning up against several of the trees. He opened one up, and a hint of vinegar, like they had smelled at the germplasm bank, wafted out.

Don Fernando explained that he tried to do fermenting and drying correctly. That is why he had invested in and built out his processing station. But it just didn't make economic sense. It was too much work for no reward.

A buyer from Jaén came out to the farm every couple of weeks to buy Don Fernando's cacao, and it didn't matter to the buyer whether the cacao had been dried on the table or the farm floor. The buyer also didn't care one bit about how the cacao was fermented.

The only metric of interest to the buyer was how dry the cacao was. If it had been under the sun for three or four days and covered when it started to rain, and if it had hard shells, that was enough.

Brian asked whether the buyer cared about the bugs and animals in and around the cacao while it was drying. Don Fernando said that apparently it didn't matter because it never held up a sale.

It was a shame. Don Fernando had invested money and time to build the fermentation box and drying table and would happily do the processing in a better way if it would lead to higher prices. But it didn't. So he would continue to ferment the cacao haphazardly in plastic bags and dry it on the ground. This freed up his time to focus on other work.

At the end of the day, Brian and Dan thanked Don Fernando and his wife deeply and sincerely for their time and the tour. As the truck pulled away, they looked back and saw the two farmers, husband and wife, at the entrance of their big, beautiful, productive farm, smiling and waving.

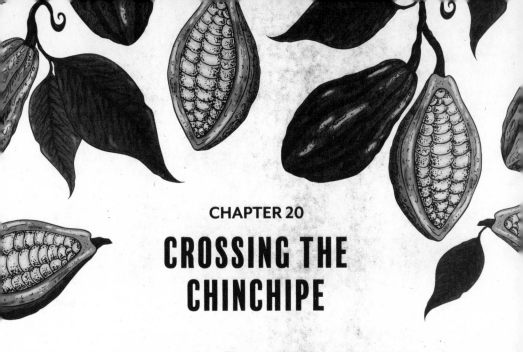

CHAPTER 20

CROSSING THE CHINCHIPE

O
n the long bus ride out of Jaén, back over the Andes, due west for the coast, then east back into the Andes along a different route to Cajamarca, Dan and Brian had a lot of time to talk and think.

They weren't clear about what to do next. They could see that buying fruits and vegetables for the mine wouldn't work. And it seemed like there were a lot of cacao farmers who wanted to do things a different way.

After many hours of brainstorming, they agreed they needed to get back to Jaén as soon as possible. They had to talk to more farmers. They wanted to see the nitty-gritty on a larger scale. They wanted to walk around more farms, meet more families, hear about their challenges, see the roads, see the infrastructure, feel the hard rain, and be inside as many cacao orchards as possible.

They were also itching to go see about the special cacao Noé Vasquez had mentioned in such a sly way.

After seventeen hours on buses, Dan and Brian finally arrived back in Cajamarca. It felt like a completely different world. Cajamarca was so tame and orderly compared to Jaén. The weather was cool and fresh, not oppressive like the heat east of the mountains. Gone were the long stretches of wild, green farmland.

Back home, Brian saw his daughter, Amara. In just a few days, as babies do, Amara had grown and changed. Holding the little girl in his arms, Brian immediately felt a pang of regret and fear. How could he have gone away? He had missed so much in just a few days. What else was he going to miss by going down the path he was now thinking of going down?

When Amara went to sleep, Brian and Ceci had a long talk. Brian admitted to Ceci that being back home was giving him second thoughts about becoming a road warrior again and that maybe he would try to get a job at the mine.

Ceci explained that the mine was shrinking. The company couldn't bring any new land under production because of their social miscues. Little by little the land currently being mined was running out of gold. A job at the mine was highly unlikely.

After a few days back, Brian fully accepted the reality of his situation. He had no choice but to hit the road. On the evening of their fourth day back in town, Brian met with Dan at his hotel and announced that he'd made up his mind. He was ready to go back to Jaén as soon as possible. Dan said that he could be ready anytime. Brian told Dan that he was going to put things in order and could leave in two days.

The next two days were tearful and tense. Brian spent as much time as possible holding and caring for Amara. When the time came to head to the bus station, Brian picked up Amara and kissed her one last time. He hugged Ceci and kissed her goodbye. He grabbed his bags and, at the door, looked back at his new wife, standing in the kitchen, holding his baby daughter.

In these moments, the best course is quick, decisive action. Otherwise, it's too easy to linger on in your desire to stay. Brian blurted out, "Te amo" ("I love you"), opened the door, and walked out.

While Dan waited for Brian at the bus station, a third traveler made an appearance. It was my brother-in-law, Nery's youngest brother, Miguel. He was twenty years old and newly graduated from journalism school. He spoke passable English.

Brian wanted to bring a translator along for Dan. It was going to be too much of a burden to look at cacao farms, think, take notes, accumulate financial data, and talk with cacao farmers while translating every single conversation as he did on the first trip.

Brian had reached out to me a few days before the trip to see if I knew of a good translator. Miguel was living in Chiclayo at the time. Brian called him and he was available.

The three travelers boarded the bus and settled in for the seventeen-hour trek to Jaén, down the western face of the Andes to the coast, through the bone-dry coastal deserts, up across fertile mountain farmland, down the dead rain shadow on the eastern side of the pass, along twisting river valleys, and back out into the jungle.

In Jaén early the next morning, a taxi pulled up in front of the hotel. Dan, Brian, and Miguel climbed in and the driver took off through the manic streets. Soon, they were out of the city, heading east. After half an hour they turned north on the Jaén-San Ignacio highway.

If you follow the Jaén-San Ignacio highway north long enough, it will take you all the way to Ecuador. It is a principal highway in the region, rolling through some of the most breathtaking jungle farmland you've ever seen.

The three men marveled at the unending procession of farms, separated by huge rolling hills painted vibrant green by dense plant life. They watched in awe, struggling to come to grips with the size and beauty of the landscape.

An hour into the trip, the taxi came to an abrupt halt. Brian looked out the window and saw they were in a traffic jam twenty cars deep. This seemed impossible. A traffic jam out on this remote road? Brian asked the driver what was going on. The driver said, "Vacas" ("Cows").

Cow after cow plodded by with no sense of urgency. Finally, an old woman wearing a cowboy hat and wielding a long stick for motivating her herd walked by. Brian watched as the herd and their elderly shepherd crossed the road into a field and the cars started moving again.

The taxi drove full speed for fifteen minutes until it was again forced to come to a complete stop. The group found themselves in another line waiting to move.

Out in front was a long, sharp curve that wheeled off to the right, hugging a big, round green hill. The road disappeared back behind the hill and could no longer be seen.

Brian asked the taxi driver why they had stopped again. The driver said, "Donacion" ("Donation").

He explained that this curve used to be very dangerous. It is a blind curve, perfect for robbing freight trucks. Robbers would stand in the road with guns. When trucks rounded the curve, a group of criminals would stand in the road pointing guns straight at them. If the driver kept going, the gang fired a warning shot into the windshield. If the driver still didn't stop, the gang would shoot to kill.

Eventually, trucks started carrying a second driver with a firearm. This led to deadly shootouts. The criminals worked for the local mafia, and the mafia started carrying out revenge hits in Jaén to put fear into the hearts of the drivers. Drivers became so afraid that they stopped resisting. This was very bad for the local economy. The mafia controlled almost all exports out of the region, and the community suffered. This went on for decades.

When a long border war between Ecuador and Peru finally settled down, many military veterans lived in and around Jaén. They became fed up with the criminal activity and decided to band together and put an end to it. They got out their military gear and formed a vigilante militia. With no authority from the local government, the soldiers showed up and started hunting down criminals.

Within six months, trucks were able to drive safely around the curve. Now, whenever anybody drives through, they stop and give voluntary donations to members of the militia. The militia has a checkpoint on the side of the road. They investigate cars. They are friendly, and everybody gives them something. This keeps the roads safe and free from robberies.

The taxi crept along until it was at the checkpoint. Ten men wearing tight, black T-shirts, camouflage pants, and bulletproof vests, with machine guns slung over their shoulders, stood in the road stopping every car that drove by.

A middle-aged soldier with long black hair, wearing a red headband, stuck his head into the back window of the car, flashed a huge smile, and called over the rest of the troop. Suddenly, all ten vigilantes poked their heads in the windows to get a look at Brian and Dan, their guns clanking against the taxi doors as they bent down to see better. Brian spoke to the militiamen in Spanish and explained that the group was going to the district of Huarango to look at cacao. The vigilante gang seemed to appreciate that.

Brian fumbled around in his pocket for a bill to donate and came up with a twenty-soles bill, about six US dollars. The soldiers were satisfied. They thanked Brian heartily while waving the taxi driver on.

Soon after the checkpoint, Dan, Brian, and Miguel got their first look at the Chinchipe River, a river that was soon to play a constant role in Brian's life. The taxi driver pointed to the river off to the right and told his passengers that they would soon arrive at the crossing.

As soon as he made that comment, the ride turned helter-skelter. The driver started weaving in and out of debris on the road. The group looked out and saw the pavement had ended, and they were now driving on dirt and jagged gravel. Brian spotted broken pieces of black asphalt pushed off to the side of the road and asked the driver why the road had fallen apart. The driver said, "Lluvia y mala construcion" ("Rain and poor construction").

After forty-five minutes of bumps and jerks, the taxi turned right and drove downhill toward the bank of the Chinchipe.

A long line of cars was backed up almost onto the main road. The driver let the group know that they had arrived at Chuchuasi, the river crossing. Brian, Dan, and Miguel could feel free to get out, stretch their legs, and look around. It would be a while until it was their turn to cross the river.

The three walked down the turnoff toward the Chinchipe. They heard the strong, rushing river, the whiny grind of outboard motors, and yelling. On their left was a tall, sheer cliff made of gray rock that extended up forty feet. The main road they were just on continued up and over that cliff toward Ecuador.

There were dozens of long canoes with outboard motors taking travelers back and forth across the murky, wide river. The current was too powerful between the two landings to cut straight across. Instead, canoes let the current carry them downriver a couple of hundred yards to a place where the current lost steam. The expert drivers made a U-turn around the weak point, and headed back upriver to the other landing, where customers paid and deboarded.

There were two gray, square floating platforms, each big enough to hold three taxis. The barges had enough room for a couple of dozen travelers plus the taxis. People climbed on and filled the spaces around the vehicles.

The two platforms had thin wires on their sides that ran up to metal cables. The thick metal cables were strung through the air about twenty feet above the river. On one side, the thick cables were held by fasteners dug into the sheer cliff. On the other side, the fasteners were dug into the road that ran through the small town on the opposite side of the river.

The two barges moved in opposite directions, propelled by nothing but the current. The cables were strung at angles that allowed the platforms to move slowly across with the flow of the river. When the barges arrived ashore, the vehicle drivers started their motors and drove off.

The very first time my dad, brother, and brother-in-law crossed the Chinchipe River on a platform barge.

The town on the other side of the river was Puerto Ciruelo. *Puerto* means "port," and *ciruelo* means "plum." One of the founders of Puerto Ciruelo was well known for growing delicious red plums. The plum trees could be seen from the river, and thus the town's name.

On the Puerto Ciruelo side, families bathed on a small beach. Beyond the bathing families, women washed clothes in the river by hand. Even further up the river were two taxi drivers using river water to wash their taxis, which were parked on the beach.

All along the river on the Puerto Ciruelo side were humble, gray brick houses with metal roofs. The houses faced a street that ran through town. The backs overlooked the Chinchipe and almost all had tall balconies supported by pilings, thirty and forty feet high, that reached down to the riverbank. Despite the balconies' rickety look, many people were out on them doing chores.

Behind Puerto Ciruelo was a vast jungle boxed in by tall mountains forming a triangular perimeter around a big jungle canyon. In the canyon, there were roughly eighty small farming villages accessible by a labyrinth of roads running from Puerto Ciruelo into the canyon's interior where cacao grows.

After about an hour, it was time for Dan, Brian, and Miguel to make the crossing. It is one thing to judge the movement of a river from the safety of the shore. It is another to look down at the powerful, rushing current when you are standing just two feet above it on a thin platform loaded down with cars and people. The platform rocked and swiveled as the water gushed by.

Once the cars and people had boarded, the captain pushed the platform away from the shore with a long wooden oar. Brian and Dan looked up and down the river, and in both directions, the river snaked and disappeared behind green jungle mountains. There was a whirlpool just in front of the spot where the motorized canoes made their turnabout.

The barge floated slowly up to the Puerto Ciruelo landing. The captain stuck out his oar to grab the dock and pulled the barge flush with the shore. A worker on shore reached out and grabbed a rope furled on a corner of the barge. He tied it to a metal post, and the passengers started climbing down.

The cars drove ashore and turned right, down a sleepy six-block road that constituted the entire downtown of Puerto Ciruelo. Brian, Dan, and Miguel walked behind their taxi onto the road.

CHAPTER 21

HUARANGO

There they stood on a sidewalk in a tiny town in the middle of the northern Peruvian jungle. Locals streamed out of their homes and workplaces to get a look at the strangers.

Time dragged on. Neither Brian, nor Miguel, nor Dan had a good idea about what to do next. Just as Brian thought about yelling out, asking if anybody knew Noé Vasquez, Noé broke through the crowd with a small delegation, including several of his cousins and brothers and the mayor of Puerto Ciruelo. They all came speeding toward the group, reaching out for handshakes.

Noé gave an exuberant smile and grabbed Brian's hand tightly. He then pulled on Dan's outstretched hand, and the cousins, brothers, and mayor all jumped into the fray, greeting and hugging their visitors.

Noé motioned to Dan, Brian, and Miguel to follow him to a nearby cantina for a celebratory beer. Inside the empty cantina, the group sat near a window overlooking the river and shared a single, big bottle of cold beer.

Five years later, Anthony Bourdain and Eric Ripert would drink a beer with Dan in this same cantina while shooting their Peru episode of *Parts Unknown*.

Our long-time business partner, friend, and cacao savant, Noé Vasquez.

Amid a crowd of onlookers, Brian, Dan, and Miguel made their way out of the cantina and back to their taxi. Noé gave the driver directions to his farm in the village of *Cigarro de Oro,* "The Golden Cigarette."

A moment later, a caravan of motorcycles flew by with Noé and the mayor on the back of two of them. They all climbed the hill out of Puerto Ciruelo and drove through a canyon on narrow, winding dirt roads barely wide enough for two cars to pass.

It was quiet in the canyon except for birds calling, dogs barking, chickens clucking, turkeys gobbling, cows mooing, and the rush of strong winds through the leaves. Farms were on either side of the road, and the vehicles had to drive slowly to avoid the animals, especially the riled-up dogs running back and forth.

From the taxi, they saw shaded orchards. Tall trees with big leaves provided a canopy for the other plants underneath. Inside the orchards they saw brightly colored, oblong cacao pods hanging from sturdy, angled branches.

They saw men with wicker baskets hung over their necks, walking barefoot, scraping coffee cherries off the thin branches of squat coffee bushes.

Occasionally, they passed open clearings where all the bushes and trees had been cut. In these spaces, families were hard at work in rice paddies, their bare feet submerged in puddles of water up to their shins. The rice farmers were hunched over, pulling bunches of what looked like tall green grass out of the muddy ground.

After twenty minutes of slow driving, the caravan crossed over a beat-up, jury-rigged bridge straddling a healthy creek tumbling over big gray-and-black rocks. Shortly beyond the bridge, the caravan turned down a rocky driveway and parked.

Noé motioned for the group to follow him to his house. The house was built of wood planks with a tin roof, typical of the area. A concrete porch ran along one side of the house with wooden chairs for guests.

From the porch, the view was pure farm. There were trees and animals everywhere. Ducks waddled up to Brian, Dan, and Miguel and then waddled away. Turkeys came gobbling around, panhandling for scraps of food. Dan pointed up at a tree heavy with big, yellow coconuts.

An older woman with a strong, assertive presence came out. When she smiled, the sun glinted off the silver cap on one of her front teeth. She had thick black hair and eyebrows and, in most ways, appeared to be an older, shorter, female version of Noé. It was Noé's mother. She had come to invite the group in for lunch before they toured the farm.

While everyone ate, Noé took it upon himself to give an impromptu history lesson. He started by saying that the district of Huarango was very new. It was only in the last fifty to sixty years that people had moved into the canyon to live and farm. When the government started taking land away from the aristocratic land-owning families in the 1960s and putting the land under the control of campesino communities, it was the catalyst for homesteaders to move in.

Adventurous souls from all over northern Peru came to stake their claim. People came from Cajamarca, Piura, Chiclayo, Chota, Trujillo, and other northern cities to settle onto their very own piece of land. It was well known that the land outside Jaén was excellent for farming.

When people first came, they found raw nature, roaming members of the Pakamuros tribe, who lived near the Chinchipe River, and scattered settlements of the Awajun tribe, who had built small communities deeper in the canyon.

At first, the new landowners weren't even sure how to cross the Chinchipe. They had to find sticks floating in the river to build rafts. It was very dangerous.

On the other side of the river, people were greeted by wild animals—jaguars, bears, and bobcats. The original settlers had to carry rifles or machetes, and it was common to use machetes to fight a wild animal to the death. Eventually, people cleared their plots of land, settled in, and started farming and living together in small communities.

After lunch, in the sweltering early afternoon heat, Noé and the group hiked across fifteen acres of dense vegetation to a grove where Noé kept a special collection of cacao trees.

Inside the shady cacao orchard, Noé motioned the group over to a log on the ground. The top half of the log had been sawed off so that it could be used as a small table or staging platform. Noé asked one of his brothers to cut down ripe cacao pods.

Dan and Brian watched Noé's brother walk over to a tree loaded down with bright yellow and green cacao. With swift, expert motions, he used his machete to hack through the thick stems from which the pods hung. After cutting down about ten green pods and letting them fall to the forest floor, Noé's brother scooped them all up and brought them over to the flat log.

One by one, Noé cut each of the pods in half, slicing through both the pod and the seeds inside. He laid out the half pods next to each other. Noé then gestured for everyone to kneel down and get a closer look.

Dan and Brian had torrents of sweat running down their faces. The forest floor was covered with black muck so deep that the actual earth could not be seen. Birds squawked and insects hummed. Other than the ambient noise, everything was quiet. Dan and Brian were laser-focused.

Immediately, Dan saw something different about this cacao. Some of the seeds inside were white. Dan mentioned this to Noé, and Noé smiled, patted Dan on the back, and congratulated him for having such a good eye. Miguel translated, and then Dan asked Noé what this meant.

A pure Nacional cacao pod cut in half to see the color of the seeds. The darker seeds are bright purple and the lighter seeds are creamy white.

Noé explained that this cacao was the *criollo* cacao of the area. Criollo is a catchall word in Peru meaning "original, heirloom, or authentic." Criollo is also a genetic variety of cacao, but that isn't what Noé meant. Noé meant that this cacao was native to the canyon.

To Noé's eyes, it was the most beautiful cacao in the world. The aesthetics of the tree, the shape, color, and size of the pod. The texture of the husk. The ridges. The taste and vibrancy of the mucilage. It all struck him as perfectly crafted by millions of years of adaptation to its environment. It was from Huarango. It was a jewel of nature.

As to the white cacao, Noé didn't have a good explanation. He only knew that it was uncommon. For example, the other trees in his collection didn't have this characteristic. But all over Huarango, on all the farms, the criollo trees had white cacao, and Noé found it fantastic.

Dan asked Noé what the average percentage of white cacao was in the pods, not just on his farm but throughout the canyon. Without a moment of thought, Noé responded that 40 percent of the cacao in the criollo pods was white. To prove his point, he pointed down at the cut pods and started counting. Forty percent was the precise count.

Dan looked around at Noé, Brian, Miguel, the cacao orchard, and the farmland around them. Something about that number, 40 percent, struck him as special. Dan felt sure that they'd come all the way out to Huarango to hear that number. Forty percent white cacao.

As the afternoon wore on, the gang hiked around other parts of the farm. They saw more plants and heard more history. It was a magical experience from beginning to end, and they were sad for the day to wind down. Eventually, they climbed into the taxi, floated back across the river, drove back down the broken road, tipped the vigilantes again, and returned to Jaén.

For the next several days Dan, Brian, and Miguel toured Shanango, San Lorenzo, San Agustin, La Foresta, and Shumba Alto, cacao-growing communities along the Jaén-San Ignacio road south of Chuchuasi, Huarango, and the Chinchipe crossing. They took a second trip out to Huarango and saw other farms, with Noé as their guide. The white cacao counts lived up to Noé's claim.

Every community they visited had come to essentially the same conclusion. Individual farmers in the region would never have the capital or time to ferment and dry cacao well enough to make fine-flavored chocolate. And if they couldn't sell into a fine-flavored cacao market, they were doomed to receive rock-bottom prices for their cacao.

This would inevitably lead to more and more farmers planting high-volume industrial hybrids. Given a low price, the only play is volume. Unfortunately, the industrial hybrids exact a price from the soil. The higher production depletes the nutrients in the soil and starts killing off everything around it over time.

Eventually, chemical fertilizers are needed to revitalize the soil. This adds an extra cost that nullifies the benefits of high-volume production. In a state of poverty, when you are trying to survive day to day, there is strong pressure to look at things in the short term.

The farmers didn't want to be caught up in this vicious cycle. The practical solution was centralized processing. Somebody needed to come in, buy wet cacao from the farmers, and do the fermenting and drying themselves. They could sell the resulting cacao at higher prices and, in turn, pay the farmers more.

Brian was going to be the operations man on the project, and he felt he grasped the fundamentals. There were big obstacles to overcome and important questions to answer. First and foremost was whether the cacao in this region could be considered fine flavor if processed correctly. Could they fetch a premium price even under perfect conditions?

The other problem, and it was a doozy, was that Brian didn't have the slightest idea about how to ferment and dry cacao. He could do research and try to learn, but research and reality are very different things.

Despite the uncertainties and unanswered questions, Dan and Brian were completely swept away by their trip to Jaén, and especially by Noé,

Huarango, and the white cacao. On the long bus ride back to Cajamarca, they tentatively decided to wade in.

Brian would draw a stipend from the company and start traveling regularly to Jaén. He would rent a small place and build sample fermentation boxes and dryer beds. He'd go out to the surrounding communities and start buying limited quantities of cacao. He'd try to produce a good result, something that could be considered fine flavored, and they'd start looking around for chocolate companies interested in buying their cacao.

Back in Cajamarca, Dan said his goodbyes to Brian and Ceci. Brian settled briefly back into family life. He helped out around the house, spent time with Amara, did what he could to chip in, all the while making plans to go back to Jaén in just a couple of weeks.

Straightaway, Dan got on a plane with Nancy and flew to Hawaii.

A big chunk of their itinerary was visiting Hawaii's cacao farms. On one such farm, Dan got to chatting with the owner about our project in northern Peru.

The farm owner was a longtime industry expert, and he told Dan that white cacao was a special and rare find. He explained that cacao seeds are purple because they are high in tannins, which cause a dry, acidic flavor profile, like red wine. White cacao has the all the chocolate flavors without the acidity. This leads to a much mellower, nuttier, more chocolatey chocolate.

He assured Dan that there would be tremendous demand for a new origin of white cacao. To be specific, this fellow told Dan that chocolate folks would get on a private jet to come see him if he had white cacao. This sent shockwaves through Dan. The magic he had felt out on Noé's farm had just been confirmed by a credible authority.

From Hawaii, Dan called Brian and told him that white cacao would have huge demand. To hell with being tentative. Dan told his partner to go all in—the company would pay for whatever was needed.

The company's money was Dan's life savings, and he was telling Brian to start spending it. At age sixty-nine, the riverboat gambler was still willing to push his chips to the middle of the table if he thought he had a winning hand.

Brian told Dan that if they were going all in, he might need some help. It wouldn't be easy to manage family life and kick the project into high gear all on his own. Brian wanted to hire Miguel.

Dan told Brian to do whatever he needed to do. He trusted Brian completely. In the meantime, Dan would start researching the market in the United States to figure out to whom we would sell cacao. That's when I got reeled back in.

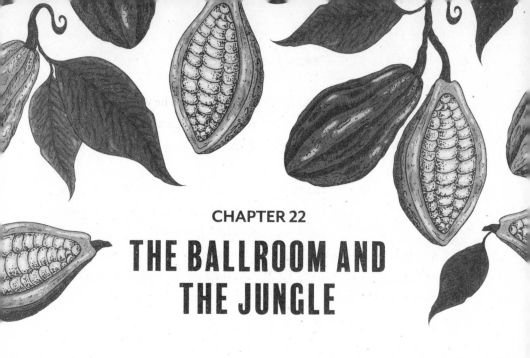

CHAPTER 22
THE BALLROOM AND THE JUNGLE

was deathly bored working for the government. It wasn't who I was brought up to be. When my dad came back from Hawaii and filled me in on happenings in Peru, it gave me hope. I still harbored dreams of working for a family business.

My dad told me that the two of us were going to start attending meetings of the Fine Chocolate Industry Association and that we'd start walking the Fancy Food Show. This meant flying to San Francisco and New York several times per year to network and attempt to make sales.

I liked the sound of that. I was eager to learn from my dad and see him in action. Just one detail needed the tiniest bit of clarification. What exactly would we be selling?

Cacao with 40 percent white beans of course! We were going to these meetings to sell the special cacao Brian was buying and processing. I pointed out to my dad that we didn't have any inventory or any idea when we'd get some. He said we'd figure it out as we went along.

While my dad and I were trying to figure out how to sell cacao, Brian toured cacao-processing operations. He visited a co-op in Ecuador. He went to a cacao-growing region not far from Jaén called Bagua, on the other side of the Marañón River. He went to Piura. He saw all kinds of processing methods and learned the theories and thinking of the people who ran the operations. He read every book he could find on the subject, from the seventeenth century through the present.

Brian and Miguel rented a room together in Jaén. It was a single room with gray concrete walls and a bathroom. That was it. They slept in bunk beds. When Brian went home every two weeks to stay with his family in Cajamarca, Miguel held down their miniscule fort.

Brian struck a deal with Sarah Parades to use a small part of the government germplasm bank for test runs on fermenting and drying cacao. Based on what he had learned during his tour, Brian drew up his own plans for how to proceed. Miguel found a carpenter in Jaén to build our first fermentation boxes and drying beds to spec.

Brian and Miguel bought a couple of motorcycles and started motoring out to buy cacao from farms in the villages surrounding Jaén. They could only buy as much cacao as could be strapped to the back of the bikes.

Huarango was one of the places they visited frequently. But it was the farthest away, and the ride out had that terrible ten-mile stretch of destroyed road.

Riding motorcycles out to cacao farms was just about the most fun and free thing that Miguel and Brian had ever experienced, even though it was dangerous. The region was entering its rainy season, and the roads were way muddier and slipperier than they expected. Their tires slipped out or got bogged down almost every trip, sometimes throwing them from their bikes. They got banged up, scraped, and torqued, head to toe.

Even so, they loved being out in the countryside, riding fast along country roads. The rivers were swollen and thrashing from all the rain, and the roaring of the rivers could be heard over the sound of their engines.

The peaks of the jungle mountains were covered by black clouds. Rain drenched Brian and Miguel as they rode. The temperature was boiling hot. The whole thing was intoxicating.

After spending the early part of the day on farms, scraping wet cacao seeds into buckets, they headed back to the germplasm bank to try their hand at fermenting and drying.

In the United States, during the week leading up to our first Fine Chocolate Industry Association meeting, I bragged to my government coworkers about how my family was going into the chocolate business and how I was going to an industry event that weekend.

They were clearly skeptical. They didn't know my dad or my brother. I had told them about my trip to Peru, how I met my wife, what an adventure it all was. They took my stories to be far-fetched and potentially fabricated. If all that was true, why was I doing payroll for the government?

The night before we flew to San Francisco, I met with my dad. We scoured the list of attendees we'd see at the event. We circled the names of people we wanted to meet with a thick red marker. My dad made me a copy of the list with the red circles, and I folded it up and put it in my pocket.

Lying in bed that night, I studied the list. I imagined myself winning over every name on it. In my mind's eye, I saw their impressed smiles when I told them about the white cacao. I pictured being peppered with questions about my brother, Brian, and his work in the jungle, and giving perfectly eloquent responses. I envisioned prospect after prospect shaking my hand, giving me their business cards, telling me, yes, we were going to do a deal. I drifted off to sleep with a smile on my face, sure of my impending success.

The reality was completely different from my musings. It took all my nerve to walk up to strangers, make a brief opening remark, then launch into my spiel. I wonder if they saw me nod to myself when I realized that the name on their tag was one I had memorized. Did they see me take a deep breath, smooth down the front of my sports coat, stand up straight, and plaster a fake smile on as I made my approach?

I wonder what they thought when I asked their take on the weather in San Francisco, nervously pretending to listen to their answer while preparing to say what I actually came over to say. I know for certain they were not impressed with my cockamamie story about discovering white cacao in Peru and how my brother was living down there trying to buy and process it.

I know this because the best I got from the first dozen or so people I approached was a polite smile, a ten-second hearing, and a "nice to meet you" as they walked away to speak with someone who actually mattered. I went zero for twelve, and my spirit was crushed. I was so excited for this. To fail so fully and so fast made me feel terrible.

Dejected, I sat down all alone at a table set for the meal during an upcoming presentation. A waiter walked by, and I asked where I could get some hot water. I was too depressed to even want coffee or a drink with any flavor. He pointed me to the coffee station. I pumped myself a cup and then went back to the table.

A few minutes later, a woman came up from behind me and asked if she could sit next to me. I said sure, and she introduced herself as Lizette. She asked what I was doing at the event, and I started telling her the whole story, not as a pitch but as one friend would tell another.

She listened with great interest and sympathy, asking questions as I went along. This warmed me up. I went all the way back to the beginning, told her about rehab, Nery, the mine, my brother, Peru, the mountains, the trout, the ethanol, and the white cacao. I laid it all on the line.

The presentation got underway, and while I ate and listened, Lizette leaned in and told me I needed to speak with Gary. I asked her which Gary she was referring to, and she said Gary Guittard. Gary Guittard? That was one of the most important names on our list. It had two red circles around it. He and Lizette were good friends.

I asked Lizette where he was. She pointed to the front of the room. He was sitting up front along with two or three others on a discussion panel. Gary Guittard is the CEO of Guittard Chocolate, a family-owned chocolate company located in Burlingame, California. The company was originally founded by a French immigrant, Etienne Guittard, and Gary belongs to the fourth generation of family members to successively run the company.

After the presentation, everybody rushed to the stage to connect with the panelists. A crowd of people gathered around Gary, and he patiently gave each person a hearing. I wouldn't have had the courage to wade in, but Lizette led me through the crowd and made the introduction. She gave my elevator pitch to Gary better than I ever could have.

Gary was a true gentleman. We chatted for a few minutes, and he told me that his company made chocolate samples free of charge for anyone with a new origin of cacao. He gave me his card and told me that when Brian sent some well-fermented cacao, he'd love to make our first chocolate samples. I thanked him profusely, shook his hand, and walked away. Lizette stayed behind to speak with Gary.

After that taste of networking success, I figured I had the hot hand. I started spying name tags again until I saw another name I recognized, Steve DeVries. He also had two red circles around his name.

Steve is a true pioneer in the American small-batch, bean-to-bar craft-chocolate movement. When we were researching attendees, we saw many quotes from people saying that Steve DeVries made the best chocolate they'd ever tasted. If he was the guy who made the best chocolate, we wanted to talk to him.

Steve was super gracious. He gave me a hearing. He asked questions. He offered to help. Steve had assisted in the founding of several successful craft-chocolate companies in the United States. He would end up helping us too, tremendously, at the beginning of our cacao journey.

While Dan and I were hobnobbing at industry meetings in the ballrooms of nice hotels, Brian and Miguel came to realize they needed to upgrade their setup. The single concrete room and the borrowed corner of government land weren't going to cut it much longer. They needed a bigger space of their own where they could live, do admin work, and process larger quantities of cacao.

They put out feelers in Jaén and ended up finding a space that had previously been used as a parking lot for taxis and motorcycles. The courtyard where the vehicles used to park was enclosed by a tall brick wall.

There was a small, filthy structure on the property that Brian and Miguel cleaned up and turned into a sleeping room and office. There was no space for a kitchen, so they set up a cooking station outdoors with a propane camp stove.

Our very first cacao processing facility was in an abandoned parking lot. Brian and Miguel slept together in the small room on site.

They transported their processing apparatus from the germplasm bank to the new location and commissioned the construction of several more fermenter boxes and dryer beds. They wanted to fill up the space so they could do a higher volume of experimentation.

Miguel and Brian were two guys living out of a single room that was burning hot all the time. It was furnished with bunk beds and a small desk. They had a tiny bathroom with a toilet they flushed with a bucket of water. They showered by scooping water out of buckets with a metal bowl and pouring it over their bodies in their small bathroom.

At night, if they needed to use the restroom, they were greeted by a frog infestation. Thirty to forty frogs gathered around the sink and toilet every night and jumped around the feet of whoever walked in. Not a nice surprise when you just want to make a quick trip to the bathroom.

They cooked and ate outdoors, usually under heavy rain that splattered off the tarp over their stove. Their little yard was filled with wooden cacao-processing equipment, sitting on top of grass that hadn't been mowed in years. For all intents and purposes, they were camping.

Every morning when Brian was in town, they drove out to farms on their motorcycles to buy cacao. When the midday heat was at its hottest, they sat outdoors, under their tarp, barefoot, in shorts with their shirts off, and dozed. Late in the afternoon, they worked on processing cacao. Brian came and went every two weeks. While Brian was gone, Miguel continued the work.

They processed lot after lot of cacao, measuring several key metrics multiple times daily. Based on their research, they concluded that the heat in the boxes, the pH of fermenting cacao, and the moisture content of the cacao on the dryer beds were the most important factors.

After about a hundred practice lots over the course of a year, they started producing consistent results. They got the heat to act predictably. They made the pH do what they wanted it to. They got the moisture content down to the levels required for export.

There was still one thing about which they had no idea: Did this cacao taste good? Brian and Miguel were eating a lot of cacao straight off the dryer beds, and it all tasted bitter and gross to them.

Raw, unroasted cacao is an acquired taste. By the time you eat chocolate, the cacao has been fermented, dried, roasted, ground up into liquid, sloshed over heat to remove bad flavors, and mixed with sugar, milk, or other ingredients. Finished chocolate is a far cry from dried cacao straight off a dryer bed. They didn't know what to think.

Brian knew that the cacao had to be top notch if we were going to sell it into the fine-flavored chocolate market. He didn't want to embarrass himself or us by sending something that didn't measure up. He decided to take a sample of cacao to a flavor-testing lab in Piura to get an opinion.

This was a nerve-racking experience. Brian had been leaving his family behind and coming out to Jaén to process cacao for almost six months. He'd been spending company money on rent, paying himself and Miguel, and buying cacao. If the cacao score came back bad, then what?

Brian's worst nightmare came true. The flavor scores came back terrible. Low marks on almost every metric. The cacao was poorly fermented. It was nowhere near good enough to make high-quality chocolate. Under these circumstances, Brian felt there was no basis for our continued participation.

In retrospect, the outcome shouldn't have been such a surprise given that Brian started with zero knowledge and experience. It was still a huge blow. Brian's confidence and motivation were shot, and he didn't know what to do next. The only thing he could do was call Dan and me to see if we had any ideas.

In fact, we did have an idea. Steve DeVries had offered to help. In addition to being an expert chocolate maker, he had also worked extensively in Costa Rica helping cacao farms improve their postharvest processing. My dad gave Steve a call and worked out the details. Steve agreed to come to Peru and see what Brian was doing. This would prove to make all the difference in the world.

CHAPTER 23

FINDING THE MOTHER TREE

We'd been telling people we had discovered a source of *criollo* cacao. This turned out to be a mistake—an honest mistake because we were newbies—but it was misleading. The farmers who sold us their cacao referred to it as "criollo" in the sense that it was the native, original variety from the area.

However, there is also a very fine genetic cacao variety called *criollo*, well known for growing in Venezuela. It also has white seeds and makes very delicious chocolate. The supply is limited, and the idea that there was genetic *criollo* cacao growing elsewhere was an exciting prospect. But we didn't want to mislead people. In fact, we were eager to know the true genetic variety of the cacao we were buying.

Dan started researching genetic testing on cacao. He found that the USDA had two facilities on the east coast with labs doing genetic classifications of cacao. One was in Miami and the other in Beltsville, Maryland. Dan called the Maryland lab and followed the prompts to speak with the genetics lab. A man answered. It turned out that this man's secretary was out sick, and he was answering himself in her absence. He was Dr. Lyndel Meinhart, lead researcher of the agriculture genetics testing lab. He was also a good old Midwestern boy from Missouri. Lyndel and Dan hit it off immediately.

Dan laid out the purpose of his call. We'd been doing business in Peru for more than six years, first in mining, and now in cacao. Outside of Jaén, near the Marañón River, we'd been invited to a canyon separated from the main road by a river called the Chinchipe, where we'd been shown cacao with 40 percent white seeds.

Dan explained that his business partner was in the region buying cacao and learning postharvest processing. We were buying from all over the zone, but in particular we were very interested in this white cacao, which the farmers referred to as "criollo." It would be helpful to know the real genetic variety. The purpose of his call was to learn how to do genetic testing on cacao.

Lyndel paused and absorbed what Dan had said. He had been working with cacao for a very long time. His wife was Brazilian, and he had extensive experience testing cacao throughout South America. He'd never heard of any white cacao growing near Jaén. It sounded very interesting and mysterious. Lyndel asked Dan to describe the landscape in more detail.

Dan explained there were tall jungle mountains coming off the Chinchipe forming a triangular canyon. He told Lyndel about the history of the region. He explained how a labyrinth of roads led from the port town back into the canyon where there were eighty or so little villages. Dan described the agroforestry farms with all kinds of trees and plants growing side by side. He told Lyndel about the red cacao pods, the industrial hybrids, and the yellow pods with white cacao which everybody said were native to the region.

When Dan finished, Lyndel offered a hypothesis. Midges, small flies that cross-pollinate cacao trees, cannot cross rivers or fly over tall mountains. That canyon created a microclimate and an isolated environment.

Without outside pollination, plants growing wild in that canyon would be inbred. Family members have no choice but to procreate with one another. Just like with humans, this creates deformities. White cacao is the result of long-term inbreeding. It signifies that a population of cacao has grown in isolation for a very long time.

To find out the genetic variety, they would need to collect leaf samples from throughout the canyon to analyze their DNA. Given the extremely interesting context, Lyndel said that he'd be willing to authorize a budget to carry out genetic testing on cacao from the canyon.

Dan expressed his appreciation and asked what the next step was. Lyndel explained that Brian would need to go out and collect leaves. This required plucking leaves from cacao trees, putting them in ziplock bags with desiccant inside, and sending it all to Maryland via DHL.

Brian and Lyndel did a phone training, and soon thereafter, Brian headed out to the district of Huarango to do the collection.

But before Brian could collect any leaf samples, Steve DeVries came down to get a look at Brian's fermenting and drying processes. After several days traveling around to cacao farms, observing and analyzing every step beginning to end, Steve found two principal problems with Brian's methods.

First, Brian had overengineered his fermentation process. Brian had a solid goal—he wanted uniformity in fermentation. His desire was for every cacao bean in the box to have equal exposure to heat, oxygen, and yeast. Brian's methodology for achieving this was to manually rotate sections of cacao from one place to another inside the box.

He attempted to use color-coded buckets outside of the fermentation box to achieve his goal. Daily, he and Miguel rotated cacao from one part of the fermenter box to another. The bottom level went to the top, and every other level moved down. This way, he thought, he was able to achieve part of his goal, uniformity.

Unfortunately, the cacao was uniformly terrible. One problem with taking cacao out of the fermentation boxes and putting it in buckets while levels were rearranged was that the cacao got cold. Cold cacao doesn't ferment completely, which leads to overly acidic, bad-tasting chocolate.

Steve pointed out that Brian suffered from a logical fallacy. He was falling prey to the idea of false precision. Just because you create a strict process doesn't mean you are being precise. What needed to happen was uniformity through randomization. Instead of making sure each cacao seed had equal time and exposure to each part of the box, it would be better to create a probability distribution whereby any cacao bean could be anywhere in the box at any time.

To make this happen, Brian and Miguel started taking all the cacao out of the fermentation boxes every day and putting it into tall, wide barrels. They hand mixed the cacao altogether thoroughly, then put it back in the box. If they did this quickly enough, the cacao didn't cool, and they were able to get a complete ferment. Mixing cacao in this way also aerated it. This gave the aerobic portion of fermentation the air it needed to get the cacao nice and hot.

The second important insight from Steve was that it isn't good to put fermented cacao straight under the sun to dry. Brian was aware of this problem but didn't have a good technique for remedying the issue. When cacao is put under the sun to dry after fermentation, a membrane that surrounds cacao seeds dries into a brown, brittle shell that traps flavors inside the seed.

Fermentation creates a lot of vinegar and alcohol. Cacao is drenched in these flavors and aromas after fermentation. Going straight out to the dryer bed traps these undesirable flavors and they will show up in the chocolate. You can cover them with vanilla and a ton of sugar, but if you want a fine-flavored chocolate, you need to be able to taste the cacao. If the cacao is vinegary, the taste of the finished chocolate is much less fun.

Steve recommended a resting period between fermentation and drying that should take place in a cool, shaded room. We came to call this a pre-dry. Brian had already attempted a pre-dry, but he wasn't doing it in a cool enough location. The way Brian was doing it, the cacao had too much exposure to the sun. Based on Steve's insights, Brian designed a process that could scale operationally, and he ran with it.

Over the coming months, Brian and Miguel practiced postharvest processing with their new knowledge. Once they felt able to produce consistent results, they took a new sample to the flavor lab in Piura. This time the cacao received extremely high scores on every metric.

When Brian called us with the news, his excitement was palpable. It had taken him nine months and hundreds of attempts. He had gone back and forth repeatedly between Cajamarca and Jaén, leaving his baby daughter and wife behind. He and Miguel had driven out to cacao farms every day on motorcycles in the rain. They had slept on bunk beds in a hot concrete room in the jungle. But they had figured it out.

When Brian told Noé Vasquez about the genetic testing project, Noé insisted that Brian collect samples from a particular farmer's property. It got even more specific than that. There was one tree out of tens of thousands in the canyon that Noé was enamored with.

That tree was on the farm of Don Fortunato Colala. Don Fortunato has a lovely, sprawling cacao farm, and Brian went out to Don Fortunato's farm to prepare half a dozen samples. Noé went with him, and when they came to the special tree, Noé made Brian stop to look at it. To Noé, it was the most perfect cacao tree in the world. The shape of the pods and the way they hung. The thickness and angles of the branches. The height. The shape of the leaves. Its productivity.

Noé had looked at this tree dozens of times, and it always made him take a moment to ponder how magical nature could be. If nature could produce such a perfect tree, she must be very powerful and meticulous.

Noé pleaded with Brian to take a specimen from this tree. It was the fourth sample that Brian took from Fortunato's farm. Over the next several months, Brian visited many farms and included dozens of trees in the testing.

Don Fortunato Colala and his lovely wife, Elena, next to the Fortunato No. 4 mother tree.

It's hard to forget the day we received the genetic testing results from the USDA. It was on my mom's birthday, August 7, 2009. Lyndel called my dad on his office phone. When Dan answered, Lyndel asked him if he was sitting down. Dan said, no, he wasn't sitting down because he was changing his clothes to go out. Lyndel told Dan to stop doing what he was doing and have a seat. There was exciting news to share.

Dan's heart started pounding fast. He sat down with his shirt halfway unbuttoned and no socks on as Lyndel laid out the astonishing information he had called to share. The samples that Brian sent in were pure Nacional cacao.

Nacional was a prized variety of cacao thought to have been completely wiped out by disease more than a hundred years earlier. Until the early 1900s, Nacional was used in much of the very high-end, fine-flavored chocolate made in Europe. It was sought after and prized for its flavor, which was famous for including delicious fruit and floral notes.

Nacional's homeland was always known to be Ecuador until a disease that attacks cacao called witches' broom decimated it. Before witches' broom swept through at the beginning of the twentieth century, several samples of what were considered to be perfectly representative trees of the variety were saved in a germplasm bank. When the technology became available, the genomes of those trees were mapped, and those genomes were considered the profile of pure Nacional cacao.

The USDA and other international organizations had been testing trees throughout South America for decades. In Ecuador specifically, the name Nacional is still used. However, all genetic testing done on trees in Ecuador has come back as a genetic mix. Mostly, the findings have shown a blend of Nacional and Forastero, a workhorse, disease-resistant cacao, known for productivity rather than flavor.

All of Brian's samples were at least a 98 percent genetic match to the marker trees. That seemed to indicate that all the cacao trees with yellow pods, called *criollo* by the farmers in the district of Huarango, were pure Nacional cacao. However, there was one sample of the dozens that Brian sent in with an even more spectacular result.

The fourth sample sent from the farm of Don Fortunato Colala, the very tree that Noé was so strongly drawn to, came back as a 99.99 percent genetic match to the markers. That tree was the purest expression of pure Nacional ever tested. It remains so to this very day.

Dan's mouth dropped open. He looked down at the ground and put his hand on his freshly shaved bald head. His mind was racing.

Lyndel wasn't done yet. He explained that discovering pure Nacional was a big enough deal on its own, but the fact they'd come across it in Peru rather than Ecuador was remarkable. The most extraordinary thing of all, however, was the percentage of white cacao. Even in its heyday, Ecuadorian Nacional was never known to produce white cacao seeds.

Nacional cacao with 40 percent white seeds was a completely unprecedented discovery. Given how long it takes for that genetic adaptation to spread through a population, the implications were provocative. How long had this population of Nacional cacao been growing unmolested? Why was the cacao white there but not in Ecuador? Could it be that this little canyon was the origin place of Nacional cacao? Could trees have been taken out of the canyon to other places, but the native population remained alone and unbothered for thousands of years?

Dan and Brian discussed what their next move would be. Since all the pure Nacional findings had come from cacao trees in the district of Huarango, Brian thought it might make sense to leave Jaén altogether and start buying cacao exclusively in the canyon. If they decided to go that route, Brian could work with Noé to find a place where we could process larger quantities of cacao. To Brian's engineering mind, this would be efficient because the villages we'd be buying from would all be grouped together in single district, not as spread out as the villages we'd previously been buying from.

Dan liked this idea. It would cost money to build out a facility and start buying larger quantities of cacao. The company hadn't received any cash inflow since early 2007 when the mine had paid their last invoice. We were close to running on fumes, but Dan was still all in. He told Brian to go for it.

CHAPTER 24

PUERTO CIRUELO

Brian decided to set up his cacao-buying-and-processing operation in Puerto Ciruelo, the port city of the district of Huarango. This was the logical choice for a few reasons.

Puerto Ciruelo was right on the Chinchipe River. When it came time to export, Brian wouldn't have to send a big freight truck down a long, narrow, washed-out, curvy jungle road. Puerto Ciruelo's roads were in decent shape, although they did flood when it rained too hard. It would be relatively easy to get cacao from a warehouse in Puerto Ciruelo onto a platform barge to float across the river.

Also, Puerto Ciruelo had a place available for building out a good-size processing facility. It was an old, dilapidated rice mill. Some fifty years earlier, when the government was distributing land to campesino communities, many remote farming communities also received funding to build rice mills.

The other thing Puerto Ciruelo had going for it was a house available for rent. Most of the district of Huarango was farmland. There weren't any apartment buildings or unoccupied houses back in the canyon. The only structures out in *campo*, the countryside, are humble one- or two-room houses, built on farms with adobe bricks or wood from the land.

The mill Brian had his eye on hadn't been used in more than five years. It was very run down, and there was a huge rice-husk mountain behind it. The rice-husk mountain was enormous, fifty feet tall and two hundred feet long. You could hike up it and walk around on top of it. The rice mountain had expanded such that it had caved in one of the back walls of the rice mill.

There was also a terrible bug-and-rat infestation to deal with. As a rule, out in campo, anything not occupied and kept up to snuff by humans will become home to other living things. Such was the case with the old mill. And there was a ton of rusting, abandoned equipment laying around all over the place.

Brian had never managed a construction project of the sort he needed to carry out at this mill. He'd have to plan the layout of the fermentation boxes and dryer beds. He'd have to knock down some walls and rebuild others. He'd need to lay down polished concrete over big swaths of the property. He'd have to put in new drainage and plumbing. It was a daunting job, but Brian was up for it. The company would have to find a way to fund it.

With the help of Noé, Brian was able to negotiate deals to rent the old rice mill and an abandoned house. There was some pushback from the community regarding the rice mill. Not everybody was pleased that a gringo was moving into town and renting something built for the benefit of the people. However, the majority liked that the gringo planned to bring a defunct parcel back to use and that maybe he would create some jobs.

Over the course of two weeks, Brian, Miguel, and their carpenter transported the cacao-processing implements from the refurbished parking lot in Jaén to the dilapidated rice mill in Puerto Ciruelo. It was quite a scene when they floated their gear across the river on a barge. For the whole town to see, here was a gringo drifting into their world with cacao

fermentation boxes and dryer beds. Then one day, Brian turned in his keys
to the place in Jaén and moved out to Puerto Ciruelo.

His first night in town was a nightmare. The new house had an awful
roach infestation. He knew there would be some creepy-crawlies in the
house, but he wasn't prepared for what he faced that first night.

The house was a good-sized gray brick structure. Brian liked that there
was enough space for a sleeping area, a desk, and eventually, he would be
able to convert the back of the house into a storage area for dried cacao.
The inside was sparse. Just one big open room. The floor was paved with
unpolished cement, a terrible thing. The bumpiness of unpolished cement
doesn't allow you to sweep easily. The bathroom was tiny. Just a toilet that
had to be flushed by pouring in a bucket of water. The shower was just a
drain in the ground next to the toilet.

Stairs led up to the roof, which was flat and had a wonderful view of
the river and countryside. On clear nights, you could see every star in the
universe from up there. The owner had started to build two additional
rooms upstairs, but the construction wasn't complete—only the framing
had been built.

On Brian's first day living in Puerto Ciruelo, when he walked into
his new home for the first time, he heard something that made his skin
crawl. The noise caught his ears as soon as he walked in. It was coming
from the walls.

He got closer to a wall to make sure his mind wasn't exaggerating. It
was real. He heard bugs inside the walls. There were so many that the sound
of their footsteps and the fluttering of their wings were coming through the
gray brick. Brian's heart sunk to his stomach. What did this mean? Did
they stay in there all the time? Or would they come out at some point?

As a precautionary measure, Brian went to a bodega a block from
his house—a small general store selling food, toilet paper, cooking oils,

clothes, and other common household items. In this bodega, the shelves were extremely bare. This was common in the half-dozen bodegas in Puerto Ciruelo, because it was so remote. Product distributors didn't come around often.

When Brian walked in, an entire family sat in the shop watching *telenovelas*, soap operas, on a small, mounted TV. He did a classic loud throat-clearing to get attention. The husband and wife pulled themselves away from the TV to attend to the new gringo in town. Brian told them he was looking for roach spray, as much as they had. The wife said they had a few bottles and got up on a stool to look for them on a high shelf.

After rummaging around, she found six bottles. Brian asked if there was more. There was not. He bought the bottles and made a mental note to check the other bodegas the following day.

Six bottles turned out to be woefully inadequate.

Back in his new home, Brian put a mattress on the floor in the middle of the room. If the bugs were in the walls, he wanted to be as far away from the walls as possible. He was having a new bed frame custom built that was supposed to be ready the next day. For one night, he would have to sleep on the floor.

Brian set up a mosquito net over the mattress using two old chairs. Mosquito nets are important out in campo. It is hot, and the mosquitos will eat you alive. They tear up your skin, leaving you red, welted, and itchy. They also transmit dengue, which causes a dangerous, sometimes fatal, illness. You can't escape the mosquitos, but at least, you can avoid becoming an easy meal while you lie defenseless in sleep.

After securing the mosquito net under the mattress, Brian got down on his hands and knees to make sure the net didn't have any openings that roaches could crawl through. Brian felt confident the bed was sealed off. Even if he were to be surrounded by roaches, he felt sure none could get into his mosquito net fortress.

With the bed secured, Brian took four bottles of the roach spray and did some selective spraying. He coated the floorboards where the brick walls met the concrete floor. He sprayed the corners from the ground to as high as he could reach, which was about halfway to the ceiling. The room was big, and the four bottles didn't go very far. The two remaining bottles would stay with Brian inside the mosquito net just in case.

The room now reeked of roach spray, and the jungle heat was baking. Brian had brought some fans from Jaén. He plugged in the fans and lined them up so the air would blow onto his sleeping body. He knew from experience that this would provide scant relief. The fans only circulate hot air, but it's better than sweating it out in still heat.

Before settling into his arrangements for what he expected to be a stressful, mostly sleepless night, Brian went into his backpack and found a headlamp. He strapped the lamp onto his head and climbed into the mosquito net, tucking the net underneath the mattress behind him.

He figured that his best hope would be to fall asleep quickly. If he were sleeping, and if the net was truly tucked in well, he might just be able to sidestep the horrors that surely awaited him. If he slept through the horror, he wouldn't have to live it. In the morning, he could try to find a case of roach spray and coat the whole dang room.

Night befell the little jungle town. Brian could hear the rushing of the Chinchipe River. Several blocks up, the sound of dance music boomed out of a small bar that had a pool table. Nobody was in the street. Brian felt alone. He was alone in a new place with no friends. He was alone in a big, empty room. Alone inside his mosquito net, on a mattress on the floor. Alone with his thoughts. What in the hell was he doing? A chocolate business? Leaving his family for this?

Except he wasn't alone.

And he wasn't lucky enough to fall asleep quickly. Distracted by heat and thoughts, his chances of drifting off into a merciful sleep disappeared. He tossed and turned and listened. Not being able to sleep is maddening on its own. Madness is multiplied with the footsteps of thousands of little feet and the flapping and stretching of thousands of thin bug wings all around you.

Brian knew from the noise that he must be surrounded by bugs. But he wasn't forced to confront the severity of the infestation until he turned on his headlamp. He didn't want to turn on that headlamp. He fought the urge. It wouldn't help him any. He was stuck in that net until morning. Seeing the roaches wouldn't make them go away.

Eventually, he could resist no longer. Lying on his side, he turned on the light. In the illuminated room, he saw a sea of roaches covering every square inch of the floor. They were on the walls too, crawling up and falling off into the multitude.

He sat up inside his net, on the verge of hyperventilating. His fight-or-flight reflex kicked in, and he wanted to flee. Should he open the net and make a dash for it outside, stepping on and around the roaches to get to the door? What would that accomplish? There was nobody out there to save him. Nobody to give him a bed to sleep on. Nobody to take him in. Would he sleep on the sidewalk or sit on the curb all night? It had started raining, so he couldn't sleep on the roof. Besides, the roof very likely had its own terrifying nightlife and no mosquito net.

Intellectually, Brian concluded that staying in his mosquito net was the best choice. He tamped down his emotions and tried to slow his breathing. Little by little he succeeded, until he felt decent enough to lie down on his back. Lying on his back, the light shone on the ceiling. He hadn't thought about the ceiling. It was covered in monsters—four-inch-long cockroaches congregating and clinging just above him.

His breathing became more frantic after seeing the behemoths on the ceiling, and he was about to start crying. Just then, one of those big monsters lost its grip and fell onto the top of the mosquito net. Then another. Brian looked away, only to see that roaches had started to crawl up the side of his net.

In a spasm of fear and desperation, Brian ripped the tops off his two just-in-case bottles and started spraying. After discharging the entire two cans, he tapped away the corpses that remained on the net with the back of his hands. He felt sure that any roach who came upon the net would now die and fall away.

Unfortunately, the roach spray in the air caused a wave of frenzy among the sea of roaches. The river still rushed. The bar kept playing its party music. Nobody in the world knew what Brian was living through.

By now, he was emotionally spent, and he accepted his fate. He turned off his headlamp, lay on his side, and was able to drift off to sleep for a few hours, in a mist of roach spray and jungle heat.

When he woke, there was a sea of dead roaches everywhere. With the arrival of morning, the surviving roaches had withdrawn into their day quarters inside the walls.

Brian spent the day cleaning. He bought every can of roach spray in town. Over the next several days, with more roach spray and deep cleaning, things improved considerably.

Brian's bed frame arrived on the second day, and he didn't have to sleep on the floor anymore. This is what my brother had to go through for our award-winning, fine-flavored chocolate to come into existence. Chocolate is only fancy at the very end.

CHAPTER 25

THE CHOCOEASY

efore moving to Puerto Ciruelo, Brian sent us a fifty-pound sack of well-fermented, pure Nacional cacao from the district of Huarango that had been processed in the Jaén facility. My dad received the cacao and stored it in his bedroom closet. This attracted moths to his bedroom and gave his entire house a funky, vinegary cacao smell.

My dad and I had to decide what to do with it. We'd been going to industry conferences telling people about our project, trying to build a network. In the back of our minds, there was always a nagging concern because we didn't actually have the product we were promoting. Now we had some but didn't know what to do with it. I suggested first and foremost we should send a small amount to Gary Guittard to have samples made. My dad agreed.

I wrote to Gary and asked him how much we should send, and he told us five pounds. We did that. Now what? My dad called Steve DeVries and told him that we had some cacao fermented according to his advice. We wanted to make chocolate. What should we do? Steve said that he'd think on it and get back to us.

A couple of days later, Steve reached out to tell us there was a German company called Netzsch that had a new machine called the Chocoeasy. The Chocoeasy was supposed to be an all-in-one chocolate-making machine. Pour roasted cacao and sugar in one side and chocolate was supposed to come out the other side.

The local Netzsch rep was a guy named Harry, and he had set up shop in Las Vegas at the headquarters of a company called Chef Rubber, a supplier of specialty items for artisan chefs and chocolatiers. At Chef Rubber, Harry was giving demonstrations of the machine for those who might be interested in buying one. Harry was looking for good cacao to use in the demonstration, and Steve offered up our cacao for the demo.

That was just fine by us. We were finally going to find out if this cacao made good chocolate.

Dan bought Steve a plane ticket to Vegas, but he himself would drive from San Diego because he was bringing the precious forty-five-pound sack of beans. A lot of time, money, and, frankly, the entire future of our business was inside that humble bag.

At Chef Rubber, Dan walked in to meet Steve carrying the sack of cacao like the treasure it was. An owner of Chef Rubber, Paul Edward, greeted them and showed Dan where to set the cacao. Paul's co-owner—his wife, Crystal—came along shortly to greet the visitors. Before making chocolate, Paul and Crystal gave Dan and Steve a tour of their operation.

After the tour, they got down to business. First, the cacao needed to be roasted. This was Steve's specialty. Paul had several big ovens on-site, and the crew chose one. Steve carefully calibrated and monitored the temperature as the cacao cooked. The warm chocolate aroma of roasting cacao filled the air.

Once Steve was satisfied with the result, the gang loaded the roasted cacao into the Chocoeasy. Harry was a good salesman, and as the roasted cacao was poured into a chute, he explained the features and benefits of the machine. The Chocoeasy was unique because it was an all-in-one chocolate-making machine.

It would winnow, meaning break the cacao into small pieces called nibs, and blow away the shells. Next, it would grind the cacao into a smooth liquid and keep the cacao liquefied with heat.

To make chocolate, cacao is ground to the proper smoothness and then extra ingredients are added: sugar; powdered milk for milk chocolate; vanilla (useful if you have poorly fermented cacao and want to cover bad flavors); extra cocoa butter for a smoother, more buttery texture; and perhaps an emulsifier like soy lecithin to help hold all the ingredients together.

After all the ingredients are fully incorporated, the mixture is *conched*, sloshed around over heat for a long while. Conching applies heat to the liquid cacao with hopes that any remaining bad flavors created back in the postharvest processing will dissipate, leaving you with something that tastes amazing, with no vinegary or acidic flavors.

Once conching is complete, the heated liquid chocolate is poured into molds and left to cool. The temperature of chocolate must be managed very carefully. The process of heating and cooling chocolate correctly is called tempering. When done right, chocolate's molecules line up in such a way that the chocolate has a beautiful shiny gloss and a hard snap. Improperly tempered chocolate settles into an unsatisfying, soft, crumbly state and easily melts on your fingers when you touch it.

Harry explained that, in normal chocolate manufacturing, each of these processes is done by a separate machine. All these machines take up a lot of space and are expensive. With this new miracle machine, anyone can start making chocolate right away, and for a fair price, too.

Harry was a pro.

After several hours, everyone congregated back in the room where the Chocoeasy was cranking away. They were drawn in as if hypnotized by the smell in the air.

It was the smell of blueberries, raisins, dates, ripe plums, cooked peaches, cotton candy, and roses. It floated in the air and filled up the Chef Rubber headquarters. It was heavenly and exquisite, the aroma of the most delicious, melted chocolate.

Dan asked Harry if there was a way to taste the chocolate at this stage. Could they turn off the machine and stick a popsicle stick in or something? Harry said this could be arranged and Paul suggested that Crystal have the first taste because she had the finest palate of anyone he knew. Everyone agreed.

Paul brought some wooden sticks for dipping. Crystal went first, and the moment the chocolate hit her tongue, her face lit up. She took the stick out of her mouth, closed her eyes, and thought for a second. Then she went back for a second dip, then a third, then a fourth. It didn't seem like she was tasting anymore. It seemed like she couldn't stop eating it. After Crystal's fourth dip, everyone else used their taster sticks, and their faces lit up, too.

Dan and Steve brainstormed late into the evening with Paul and Crystal about what to do next. The consensus was that our company should try to make chocolate on a Chocoeasy machine in small batches to start, to sell mostly to chocolatiers and restaurants.

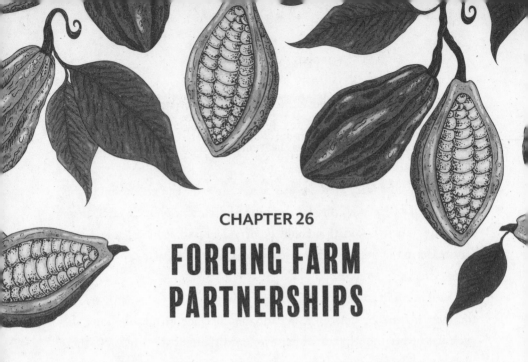

CHAPTER 26

FORGING FARM PARTNERSHIPS

Back out in the jungle, throughout the second half of 2009, Brian was making rapid progress refurbishing the rice mill. He was spending two to three weeks in the jungle, then two weeks back home. Saying goodbye to his family and the seventeen-hour bus rides back and forth never got easier. But once in campo, he couldn't help but be inspired by his work.

My brother-in-law Miguel decided to leave the company when the operation moved to Puerto Ciruelo, and Brian hired local people to help with the construction project. One was a young man named Melchiades, Melko for short.

Melko started living with Brian in his house. They had a second bed frame built, and Melko and Brian slept side by side under mosquito nets for the next ten years. (Melko still works for our company, overseeing postharvest processing. He is by now one of the best cacao processors in the entire world.) When Brian traveled home to spend time with his family, Melko kept an eye on the house and the facility.

Our first cacao processing facility in the district of Huarango
was built in an abandoned rice mill.

Brian's other main activity was convincing farmers to sell us cacao. Noé had promised that the district of Huarango was dying for a project, that the people would roll out the red carpet for us and do anything necessary to have capital investments made in the canyon. As is so often the case, the future was more lucid for the visionary leader than those who were supposed to follow.

We couldn't just show up at farms unannounced and start buying cacao. First off, farm dogs are vicious, and they'll bite the crap out of a stranger. Second, like all fruit, cacao is best purchased at a certain ripeness, which needs to be coordinated. Third, and this was the biggest obstacle, most of the cacao farmers in Huarango already had buyers.

Farmers sell products that are perishable. It is important that somebody come out on a consistent basis to buy the produce before it spoils. The farmers in Huarango had decades-long relationships with cacao buyers. It was a sure thing.

The farmers were being paid low commodity prices that kept them barely above subsistence. Even so, selling to this gringo who just showed up out of nowhere felt like a very risky proposition.

The only gringos most of these farmers had ever encountered were nonprofit types—missionaries, Peace Corps Volunteers, and wannabe social workers. All of them had come and gone. Most hadn't stayed more than a few months, a year at the most.

If a farmer were to drop off the buyer's roster and start selling to Brian, and Brian disappeared, would the buyer resume doing business with them again? Also, many buyers were relatives of the farmers. How would family members react if farmers took away their livelihoods to do business with an outsider?

Arrayed against these arguments were the much, much higher prices we were willing to pay. In addition, we would be buying cacao wet and doing the fermenting and drying ourselves. This alleviated a big burden for the farmers, freeing up their time to focus on additional crops. This had a double impact on farm revenues: higher prices and augmented production.

On top of all that was the pride of having a renowned variety of cacao growing natively in their community. Selling to the current buyers, their cacao would always be run through an industrial supply chain and treated as nothing special. The existing buyers had never done genetic testing and had no interaction with the fine-flavored chocolate market. With our project, their cacao would make world-class chocolate, a source of great pride. This was a powerful idea.

Farmers in the district feel a strong sense of pride in their land. Most people there are only one or two generations removed from the original homesteaders. Their families built up a sustainable community from nothing. It would be very honorable for their cacao to be used in a prestigious way.

However, the only way for farmers to obtain the prestige and economic benefits that Brian offered was to completely sidestep the traditional journey that cacao takes from trees in the jungle to the chocolate-consuming public.

Here is how chocolate gets to an average chocolate lover.

Cacao grows on trees all over the world near the equator. From its origin in the Amazon jungle, cacao has been exported to Africa, Asia, Central America, the Caribbean, the Pacific Islands, and Mexico.

Once cacao is cut off a tree and fermented and dried, the first of many middlemen takes ownership of it. In many places, this first player is a person in a pickup truck going from farm to farm on a fixed schedule buying cacao. In the district of Huarango, there were several warehouses in Puerto Ciruelo where farmers had to deliver their processed cacao.

Where the economy is freer, prices paid to cacao farmers will be some derivative of the world-market price, discounted so the middleman makes a profit. The price fluctuates depending on market conditions and is freely negotiated. Where the economy is less free, for example in Ghana and the Ivory Coast, which produce 60 percent of the world's cacao, prices are set by a government board. The supply chain is similar, but the pricing mechanism is different.

Most cacao farmers are economically poor, regardless of what continent they are on. At least in a freer economy, there is a way out. A company like ours can show up and offer to pay more for cacao, and farmers can choose among multiple buyers. When the government sets the price, there is no way out, and some very unsavory outcomes are the result: destruction of the natural environment and child slavery, to name just two. Very ugly.

After the person in the pickup truck or warehouse owners in small cacao-growing towns buy cacao, they drive it to the nearest big city and sell it to an aggregator.

Cacao farms are generally remote, so the nearest big city is likely a midsize town, like Jaén. The aggregator has a warehouse and freight trucks. They buy cacao from many small districts throughout the region.

Once the aggregator has enough cacao in their warehouse to justify a shipment to the capital or a big port town, they load up a freight truck and send the cacao on its way.

In the bigger town is another aggregator with bigger warehouses. They buy cacao from many midsize agricultural towns all over the country. The cacao is sold to the bigger aggregator with a markup. The cacao has now been marked up twice since being harvested and sold by the farmer.

The next buyers are huge multinational commodity brokers with offices in all the big cacao producing countries. These folks buy awesome quantities of cacao and sell it to the big chocolate makers. They arrange shipping to chocolate factories around the world.

The cacao is carried on massive cargo boats stacked high with containers. The big-city aggregators mark up the cacao and take a profit before selling to the international commodity brokers. This is the third markup.

Gigantic chocolate companies buy cacao from international commodity brokers and the brokers, of course, take a profit. That is a fourth markup.

Chocolate companies use the cacao to make their products. The factories are industrial marvels with huge machines and warehouses. There are thousands of workers and a massive shipping infrastructure.

These companies make sure there is enough chocolate manufactured so you can buy chocolate almost anywhere in the world. Supermarkets, check. Coffee shops and restaurants, check. Gas stations, check. Hardware stores, check. Airports, check. Pharmacies, check. Vending machines, check.

Once chocolate is manufactured and packaged, distributors come onto the scene. An international distributor with fleets of trucks carries away finished goods from chocolate companies.

Freight trucks transport the products to a port, where the chocolate is loaded on boats. The chocolate company takes a profit when selling to the international distributor. That is the fifth party taking a profit on the cacao.

When boats arrive at a domestic port with enormous quantities of chocolate, a domestic distributor purchases the chocolate from the international distributor, and the international distributor gets a markup. That is the sixth company taking a profit.

The domestic distributor has trucks and warehouses as well. Their clientele is anywhere someone might be hankering for chocolate. Domestic distributors deliver most of what we buy in stores. This system of production and distribution extends far beyond chocolate.

Retailers buy chocolate from domestic distributors, and the domestic distributor gets to take their profit. That is the seventh markup.

Finally, somebody goes to a store and buys chocolate to take home and enjoy. At this point, the retailer takes a profit. That is the eighth and final markup.

While in the store, customers comparison shop. This creates price competition. That's a good thing for customers. It means the system of production needs to be tight. All inefficiencies should be squeezed out so the customer gets the best possible deal.

Companies must keep their prices in line with the going rate to win your business. A chocolate company can't just arbitrarily price their products two or three times higher without justification—for example, a claim of higher quality or a great story. A higher price in a vacuum is a death knell.

What customers are willing to pay ultimately determines what a cacao farmer, worlds away on their farm, is paid.

The retail price has to embrace eight markups between the farmer and the final customer. If the price of the chocolate is very cheap, there won't be much left for the farmers. As a result, farmers find themselves in an endless cycle of subsistence living.

Campaigning with cacao farmers, Brian shared an alternative vision. What if we were to cut out all the middlemen? No pickup trucks, no aggregators, no brokers, no distributors.

Our company would buy the cacao and carry it as far as we could in the supply chain. By cutting out players, we would eliminate markups and free up money that would go back to the farmers as higher prices. By producing fine-flavored chocolate with a special variety of cacao, we'd have the justification needed to set a higher price. We'd increase the amount of money available in the supply chain and give farmers a bigger percentage of the proceeds.

Brian spent half his time putting finishing touches on our processing facility, and the other half attending cacao growers' association meetings and driving around the canyon to visit with cacao farmers.

He met with hundreds of farm families on their land. Out on farms, he ate stewed meat and *cuy* (guinea pig) with rice, yuca, and potatoes over and again. He heard about problems and learned about dreams.

My brother, Brian, gave hundreds of presentations trying to convince cacao farmers to sell us their cacao.

At association meetings, he stood up in sweltering rooms and explained how it would all work. As he looked out on the crowd, he saw farmers dozing off from the heat and the boredom of hearing the gringo make his pitch yet again. But after every meeting, a few more farmers came to Brian with questions.

As Brian learned more, he refined his operating plan. He didn't attempt to impose on the farmers a preconceived way of doing things. He created systems to suit the needs of our future partners. He trumpeted higher prices for fine-flavored cacao. Above all, he promised not to leave. He promised that we'd be there through the years. We'd never leave our partners high and dry. Over the course of several months, Brian gained traction.

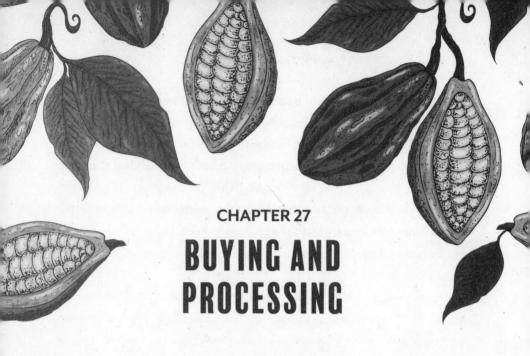

CHAPTER 27

BUYING AND PROCESSING

Back in the United States, Paul Edward shared our chocolate with many of his high-end-dessert professional friends and customers. Everybody was beyond impressed. People with decades of experience, who had tried every chocolate known to man, were telling us that our chocolate was a very exciting development. They wanted to know when it would be available for purchase. We told them we were working on it.

Based on that feedback, it felt like there was a real and ready market. Dan asked Brian to start buying and processing cacao as fast as he could. Dan wanted to fill up a full container of cacao to send to the States so that we could start making chocolate on a Chocoeasy and selling it.

Brian hired a team, and at the beginning of 2010, he got ready for our first full cacao harvest.

Coming into 2010, we truly had no idea how we were going to make, store, and transport chocolate. We just knew we had to do it. We were running out of money. Despite tremendous effort, Brian had only convinced a few dozen cacao farm families to sell to us during that first full harvest.

Brian had built our processing facility mostly on instinct. He'd learned how to process a good fifty-pound bag of cacao in Jaén, but to fill up a shipping container we'd need to process ten to thirteen tons of cacao in just a few months.

Since we didn't have enough money to pay Brian's salary, buy ten tons of cacao at premium prices, and pay our team in Puerto Ciruelo, we borrowed money from friends and family to get going.

The idea was that we'd borrow the money, buy the cacao, make chocolate, sell the chocolate at a profit, pay the money back, and hold the profits. In fact, we did that. Except we paid the money back a couple of years later than we promised. Better late than never.

Because Brian had only convinced a few dozen farmers to join the project that first year, and they didn't all live near each other, every day was a wild adventure getting out to remote farms to buy small quantities of cacao. Later on, we'd have enough farmers in a village to plan pickups for the entire village, but not that first year.

We had two separate teams, a buying team and a processing team. Each morning, both teams met up at the old rice mill to go over the day's plans. After convening, the buying team got their gear together, buckets, hand scales, plastic ponchos, machetes, goggles, shovels, first aid kits, and whatever else a person driving a motorcycle along muddy jungle roads in the rain to buy cacao might need.

Brian worked with the buying team most days in the beginning. It gave him more face time with cacao farmers. Also, he carried the cash. Unlike a lot of the buyers we were replacing, we paid cash on the barrelhead for all the cacao we bought. It was common practice for buyers to sell the cacao to the aggregator, then circle back with the money for the farmers. On top of all the other benefits, selling to us meant cash on the spot.

Somebody fell off his bike and got hurt just about every day. The team visited at least one or two farms per day that required them to leave their bikes by the road and hike across wood and rope bridges, over rushing creeks, and through thick brush. Those times, a farmer would loan the crew a donkey to haul the cacao back through the thicket and out to the vehicles.

Buying cacao in the district of Huarango means traveling
through a labyrinth of muddy, twisty, jungle roads.

Back at the rice mill, the processing team was led by Brian's roommate, Melko. The days usually started out with moving around cacao that was in the predrying stage. The team flattened and rebuilt mounds of recently fermented cacao every hour, on the hour, alerted by a digital timer.

They used custom tools that looked like wooden rakes without teeth to move the cacao. At midday, the pre-dry cacao was moved to the dryer beds and new, fully fermented, cacao came out of the fermentation boxes and was moved into the pre-dry area.

Fully dried cacao had to be taken off the raised dryer beds and put in burlap sacks. Once the dried cacao was all bagged up, a *motocarguera*, a three-wheeled motorcycle with a cargo box on the back, transported the cacao from the processing facility to Brian and Melko's combination apartment, office, warehouse.

In the afternoons, our processing team focused on fermentation. Our process required that all the cacao be taken out of every fermentation box, every single day. The team had to hand mix the cacao as fast as possible in a plastic-lined cart up on wheels, then return the cacao to the covered wooden boxes. They wheeled the cart from box to box all afternoon, scooping out fermented cacao, mixing it, and putting it away again.

Our fermentation process is very uncomfortable. You are in a room filled with bees. Bees love the sweet cacao mucilage. Recently harvested cacao early in the fermentation process drips a lot of mucilage down the sides of the wooden fermentation boxes. Bees swarm to it.

When the team takes recently harvested cacao out of the boxes for mixing, the bees firebomb the cart kamikaze style and immerse themselves in the gel. Working on fermentation means standing in a room filled with voracious bees on a sugar high and having your hands stung multiple times per day. The old rice mill had new beehives forming on the walls two or three times a week.

Cacao that is further along in the fermentation process is hot and reeks of vinegar and alcohol. The heat of the cacao adds to the already blazing temperatures of the jungle. While scooping cacao out of the boxes with buckets, our team members had to stick their faces, hands, and arms into the boxes.

The boxes need to be tall and skinny to produce the correct result, and our Peruvian team members were relatively short in relation to the boxes. Brian insisted that every single bean be taken out of the box. Not a single bean was to be left at the bottom.

This meant bending over at the waist, with the rim of the box in your gut, and sticking your head all the way down into the box to get every last bean. Having your head down in a fermentation box burns your eyes and nostrils. We tried doing this work with goggles and even snorkels brought from the United States, but the jungle heat made the swimming gear too uncomfortable to wear on a regular basis.

The mucilage on cacao turns brown, thick, and sticky later in the fermentation process. During fermentation stirs, mucilage sticks to your hands and up your forearms. It is hell to get off. After the stirs, the team had to scrape the mucilage off with a hard, flat, sharp piece of plastic.

There were a couple of hours of downtime after the stirs and until the field team came back with the day's harvest. By that time, the team had been working hard all day, and still had another three hours of work getting the new cacao into fermentation boxes.

Until the field team showed up, there was time to talk or lie down on one of the benches in the shade for a nap. Sometimes friends or family members from the neighborhood came by, and our crew played a game of pick up *futbol*.

When the sound of motorcycles could be heard coming out of the canyon and down the hill, it was time to run into the fermentation room and prepare for a flurry of activity. The radio was jacked up to full volume, and when the motorcycles pulled up, Brian and the team jumped into rapid action.

They unloaded buckets from the backs of motorcycles and taxis. The fresh, white cacao was first dumped in a wooden juicer box that was used to slough off some of the voluminous mucilage that accumulates in buckets and bags.

After the juicer box, the cacao was scooped into a mixing cart on wheels, and the team did a selection on the wet cacao. They removed rotten cacao, germinating seeds, chunks of husks, and pieces of the placenta that holds cacao seeds inside the pod.

Brian never tired of reminding the team that we were making food. Anything the team wouldn't want to eat, anything that couldn't be used for making the world's most delicious chocolate, had to come out. Most chocolate companies don't remove that stuff, and you end up eating it.

After the selection, the cacao was loaded into clean fermentation boxes and covered. A new sheet of paper on a clipboard hung from the box to track several measurements for each lot. The mixing cart on wheels was hosed down. The floor was mopped. Everything was put in order, and the day ended. Brian insisted on a culture of cleanliness in his facility. The old rice mill out in the jungle was always spotless.

This went on day after day. The campo team ventured out. The processing team took care of the cacao. Brian took the seventeen-hour bus ride home over the Andes to the coast and then back into the Andes every two to three weeks.

When your child is young, two to three weeks is a long time, and every time Brian saw Amara, she was a new little person. At home, Brian tried to acclimate himself to family life. He ate dinners with the family. He went to the park. He took Ceci on dates and tried to stir up some romance. He did admin work. He rested. After all, he was in his forties now, and hard physical labor in the jungle took its toll.

Just when he would settle back into family life in Cajamarca, it would be time for him to leave again. In Puerto Ciruelo, Brian left a manager in charge of the field team, Oscar Ayala. He is still in charge of our field operations to this day and is a wonderful, resourceful, hardworking family man. Melko kept an eye on the work at the rice mill. The work of buying and processing cacao settled into an orderly operation.

CHAPTER 28

PRECIOUS CARGO TO LIMA

Harry told us that there was a used Chocoeasy machine in Miami that we could buy. There was even a space we could rent where the Chocoeasy was all set up. That sounded good to me and my dad even though we had no experience making chocolate, no idea what on earth we were doing, and we lived in San Diego.

In April 2010, we notified Brian of our plans and asked him to prepare a shipment of cacao bound for Miami. We told him to wait no longer and to send what he had, about nine tons of cacao. Brian felt great about the quality of the cacao and what he and his team had accomplished.

My dad and I were going to fly to Miami and, with Paul's help, figure out how to make chocolate. It was a very dicey plan. Paul generously offered to help us for free in any way he could. We overdid ourselves taking him up on that offer.

Brian needed to get our cacao from Puerto Ciruelo to a seaport in Lima called the port of Callao. This meant taking our cacao across the Chinchipe on a floating platform. Then the cacao would be carried on a truck to Jaén. From Jaén, the cacao would be loaded onto a freight truck with a company who worked the Jaén-Lima route.

The Jaén-Lima route goes up through the mountain foothills and river valleys west of Jaén, over the mountains at Abra de Porculla, down the western face of the Andes, southbound through the northern desert coast, finally arriving in the mammoth city of Lima thirty hours later.

Brian hired a small, locally owned trucking company in Puerto Ciruelo with a good truck to take the cacao from Puerto Ciruelo to Jaén. Brian and the company owner agreed to get a move on as soon as weather permitted.

There were myriad details to be coordinated for the cacao to get on a boat in Lima. A phytosanitary inspection had to be scheduled. There was a lot of paperwork to submit. A date had to be booked well in advance for our cargo to be loaded on a boat. If the cacao didn't make it to Lima on time, Brian would be stranded there for several weeks with nine tons of cacao, trying to put everything back together again.

The Chinchipe River wasn't cooperating. It rained hard every day, and the river was too high to cross. The barges weren't operating. Eventually, the timeline was such that Brian was going to miss the boat, literally, if the river didn't subside the very next day.

There was another wrinkle. A rumor was circulating that, in Shumba Alta, a nearby town with an unsavory reputation for drunkenness and violence, a gang of truck thieves was holding up shipments. This was far from where the vigilante gang monitored, and therefore, each truck was left to defend itself.

Our team in Puerto Ciruelo made it clear to Brian that somebody with a gun would have to accompany the shipment. Brian had questions. Where would they get a gun? That was no problem. Most farmers have rifles for shooting wild animals. Getting a gun would be easy.

Where would the person with the gun travel? The consensus was that the gunman should travel in the "shotgun" seat up front, with the window rolled down and the gun easily visible. Potential robbers could see that the truck was armed and would be more likely to let it pass without incident.

Who would be the gunman? Everyone agreed it should be Wili. Wili was a quiet, hard worker in our processing facility. He was serious and not prone to joking and squabbling like our other young workers.

Brian asked, "Why Wili?"

Juan, Noé's younger brother, leaned in close to give his answer. Wili was nearby, and Juan didn't want him to hear. Juan told Brian that Wili would be willing to kill somebody if he needed to. Brian asked several other team members, and all assented.

Brian had a private conversation with Wili to make sure he was on board with the plan, and Wili told Brian it would be no problem at all. It was his pleasure to help. Brian told Wili to get a gun and be ready. They'd have to cross the river the very next day or put the whole thing off for several weeks.

They caught a break the next day. Brian got up early, and as he left his house in downtown Puerto Ciruelo, he asked the very first person he saw in the street how the river looked. Everyone who was awake and alive in Puerto Ciruelo knew the condition of the river at all times. The man told Brian that the river was *mediano*, "in the middle." Mediano would work.

Brian rushed to the house of the fellow who owned the truck and banged on his door. When the fellow came down, Brian told him the river was mediano and that they needed to move. The truck owner went back in to get ready. Brian ran to the old rice mill and told the team to come quickly to his home, where the cacao was stored.

The truck pulled up in front of the house, and the team started lugging out bags of cacao that weighed 110 pounds each. The fastest way is for two people to load a bag onto a third person's shoulder. The third person carries the sack to the street and throws it into the truck, where another two people organize the load. The truck had an open bed, and the team spent two hours loading sack after sack. When the loading was finished, Brian covered the cacao with a rain-resistant plastic tarp.

Now it was time to cross the river with this heavy load. When the river is mediano, it isn't calm by any means. It is still full. Whirlpools form, and people don't go down to the beach to play and swim or wash their clothes when the river is mediano. The scene was hectic.

The line forming to cross the river was long, dozens of cars deep. It had been many days since anybody was able to cross, and all who had been waiting now lined up. The canoes with outboard motors were doing heavy business taking people and small loads back and forth.

Three cars at a time drove on to the platform barges and floated across. As always, there were two barges working at the same time, floating in opposite directions, picking up and dropping off.

The line inched forward in three-car increments until finally it was our turn. In the case of a truck big enough to carry nine tons of cacao, only one vehicle could fit on the barge, ours. The barge was barely wider than the truck, and getting the truck up and over the small lip between the barge and the landing required a healthy push on the gas.

The owner was driving the truck, and he was highly experienced. He'd driven his truck onto the barge many times. It didn't make the moment less suspenseful, though. Brian watched two years of work and tens of thousands of dollars' worth of inventory drive onto the barge. The owner hit the gas and then the brake in quick succession and stopped dead in the middle of the barge. Beautiful.

Brian, Wili, and Oscar climbed onto the barge and leaned against the side of the truck. They waved goodbye to the rest of the team when the barge controlman pushed off from the landing with his long wooden oar. The team smiled and waved back as the barge floated across the mediano river.

On the other side of the river, in Chuchuasi, Wili climbed on top of the sacks of cacao in the back of the truck with his rifle. With his normal calm and determined expression, he looked like somebody who would shoot down a thief if it came to that. Brian and Oscar got in a taxi, and all started toward Jaén.

Two hours later, the group arrived in Jaén without incident. Wili didn't have to shoot anyone. They went to a depot and unloaded the cacao into a much bigger truck that Brian hired to carry the cacao to Lima. Brian and Oscar would take a bus to Lima and meet the freight truck there to oversee the rest of the process.

Our very first load of exportable cacao. The river is mediano. Wili rode on back with his gun.

In Lima, the phytosanitary inspection, which makes sure that plant life isn't carrying any harmful bacteria, was a breeze. The freight truck simply drove into a big warehouse near the port, and the necessary tests were carried out.

Brian and Oscar followed their shipment out to the port to see their cacao loaded into a shipping container. This was another example of Brian's persnickety way of doing things. He had a feeling that something bad could happen at the port, and he wanted to make sure that our cacao was treated with great care.

At the port, the stevedores who load cargo into containers were taken aback. Almost nobody ever came to watch their shipment loaded. It wasn't exactly permissible, but Brian had greased the palm of a security guard to get into the loading area. Also, the workers were shocked to see a gringo in such an industrial area.

Brian didn't like what he saw. It smelled like fish and mucky seawater on the port and unloaded cargo sat around, absorbing port odors. Brian wouldn't stand for that. He told the truck driver not to open the back door of the truck until the stevedores brought the shipping container and could load the cacao straight from the truck into the container.

Brian tipped the stevedores generously for playing along and told them all about the cacao. Blue-collar workers all over the world tend to be filled with national pride. Brian appealed to that sense of pride, explaining that Peru had one of the most special cacaos in the world growing in the north. This special cacao was in the truck. It was precious and valuable and needed to be protected. The stevedores, driven by gratuities and pride for their homeland, followed Brian's instructions.

When the shipping container showed up after an hour's wait, Brian and Oscar worked with the stevedores to load and unload the cacao using a forklift. The cacao was placed in the container according to Brian's specifications, and Brian stayed with Oscar on-site until the container was sealed. Only then did Brian consider his job to be complete.

Brian and Oscar stayed the night in Lima and, the next day, started the long trip back to Jaén. From an internet café in Jaén, Brian sent us word that our first ever shipment of pure Nacional cacao was en route to Miami.

CHAPTER 29

COME TO
THE JUNGLE

Dan got a call from Harry, the Chocoeasy guy. From the beginning, Harry's voice had that hesitant tone you use when you have bad news to share and really wish you didn't.

Harry told Dan that the Chocoeasy seller had pulled out of the deal. They wanted to keep it and take it elsewhere.

Dan screamed into the phone that our cacao had just left Peru for Miami. What were we supposed to do now?

He ended the call, furious and fuming, and decided to walk down to a cliff near his house overlooking the Pacific Ocean. Staring out over the dark gray sea, watching waves roll in and crash on the sandy beach below, he realized that he shouldn't be surprised. None of his big projects had ever come easy. Why should this one? Wasn't it absurd to think that any business venture would actually come off according to plan? Didn't the facts of life make this more likely than not? After all, wasn't his soul's evolution propelled by just this sort of moment?

This line of thought, the sound of the ocean crashing, gulls and pelicans noisily riding the cool ocean breeze, the warmth of a perfect San Diego day, all conspired to bring Dan back to an action state of mind. He needed to make a move. He went inside to call Paul Edward.

Paul tended to get salty when confronted with bad news. His basic thrust was *to hell with them*. If they wanted to pull out of the deal, they were scumbags, and they'd get what they had coming soon enough.

Dan asked Paul what he thought we should do. Paul said that the cacao was so good that we might as well take it to the best chocolate maker in the world. He advised taking a trip to see Max Felchlin AG in Switzerland.

Paul had sold Felchlin chocolate door-to-door for a long time before starting his own business. He considered Felchlin to be the finest chocolate maker in the world and had relationships with their top executives in Europe.

Dan asked what needed to happen for us to get in front of Felchlin. Paul said, first and foremost, Dan needed to speak with Franz Ziegler, one of Paul's closest friends in the world.

Franz Ziegler is a Swiss citizen, a famous and world-renowned author of cookbooks featuring chocolate and marzipan, a university professor of culinary arts, an entrepreneur, a father, a husband, and one of Max Felchlin AG's most trusted advisors. Dan asked Paul to set it up.

Within a couple of days, Dan, Paul, and Franz were on a call discussing cacao, chocolate, and business prospects. During a trip to Las Vegas to visit Paul, Franz had tried chocolate made with our cacao and thought it was excellent. He wanted to help us.

However, he had a reputation to uphold. He couldn't just back a bunch of adventurers who may prove to be nothing more than flashes in the pan. Max Felchlin AG had been around for more than a hundred years. Franz had spent decades of hard, exacting work building up his reputation as somebody who pursued excellence in every endeavor.

Interestingly, Franz's main concern was similar to that of the cacao farmers. He didn't want to work with us if we were going to disappear in a couple of years.

Dan wasn't in a position to meekly accept objections. We had cacao on the water. He threw out a crazy idea. What if they all took a trip down to Peru together? Paul and Franz could go out to the district of Huarango, meet Brian, visit cacao farms, and see the operation firsthand. They'd see for themselves that this was a long-term play.

After a brief silence, Paul blurted out that he was in. He would have to talk to Crystal, but he was in. There was another moment of silence, and then Franz said that he was in, too. Dan was stunned that his brainstorm had been accepted so quickly, but he played it cool, like it was just what he expected.

Franz, Paul, Crystal, and Dan came down to Peru in May 2010. Brian met the group in Chiclayo where they visited beaches and the famous outdoor markets. They ate traditional northern Peruvian coastal cuisine. They took the long ride over the mountains and out to the jungle.

Over the next week, the group hiked around the canyon visiting cacao farms. They rode in the back of pickup trucks through the countryside. They waited patiently as herds of sheep and cows walked slowly down the middle of jungle roads. They were treated to the warm hospitality of cacao farm families. They ate cuy and drank coconut water on Noé's farm. They saw the 99.99 percent pure Nacional tree on Don Fortunato's farm. The climbed up the gigantic rice-husk mountain behind our processing facility.

They got up and spoke at a cacao farmers' association meeting and were so carried away with the magic of the experience that they promised to make the district of Huarango the most famous cacao-growing region in the world. It was all like something out of a dream.

Above all, they were impressed by Brian's processing facility. It seemed impossible that such a detail-oriented, well-controlled, clean, meticulous operation could be built and run out in the middle of a remote jungle town.

Near the end of the trip, the group was in a restaurant in Jaén planning how to proceed. Franz suggested that Dan and Brian sell processed raw cacao to Felchlin, but Dan was against it. Our calculations were based on selling finished chocolate. Those numbers gave us the best chance to become sustainable, while also paying the cacao farmers well. Dan wanted Felchlin to make chocolate for us on a contract basis.

Franz explained that this would be a tough sell. Felchlin didn't do contract manufacturing for any US companies. They'd have to get the CEO himself to sign off on something like that. However, given what Franz had seen and experienced on the trip, he promised to help whichever route we chose.

The next topic up for debate was the name of the product and somebody had the idea of a product name along the lines of Chanel No. 5 perfume. Ideas started pouring out, and eventually, somebody spitballed the idea of Fortunato No. 4. The "4" stood for the fourth sample on Fortunato's farm. The name was unanimously acclaimed as a winner.

With Franz squarely in our camp, Dan and Paul planned to visit Switzerland as soon as the group got back from Peru.

Our container of cacao arrived in Miami, and we stored it in a warehouse until we could figure out what to do next. There was a company in Miami who could draw samples of cacao from a warehouse and ship the samples internationally. We hired them to prepare a hundred-pound sample of our first harvest and ship it to Felchlin.

While we waited for the sample bag to arrive in Switzerland, I had an experience that showed me the future in a very lucid way. After several months of waiting, we finally got our chocolate sample from Guittard Chocolate.

Inside the FedEx box, there was a handwritten note in blue ink that said, "Adam, this came out pretty good, huh? Gary." God, that little note meant a lot to me!

It was a 60 percent dark chocolate. The color was light brown, lighter than other dark chocolates because of the white cacao beans. The samples were small rectangular bars packaged in miniature ziplock bags. I could smell the chocolate through the bags.

I took a bar and handed the other bags to my dad. I took a bite of chocolate. It was transformational. Raisins, plums, cotton candy, roses. Time stopped, and I saw forever in front of me. I knew I'd be in the chocolate business the rest of my life.

My dad asked me what I thought. I told him that no matter what obstacle might be put in front of us, we were going to build a great business. How could it be any other way? It was the best chocolate I had ever tasted. I never knew that chocolate could taste like that. We weren't fine-chocolate people. We'd never been in the chocolate industry. It was all new to us. But even as a newbie, I knew that our chocolate was special.

I told my dad he should go to Switzerland with all the confidence in the world. We had the goods with this cacao. Felchlin would want to work with us. If not, we would figure it out. We always had.

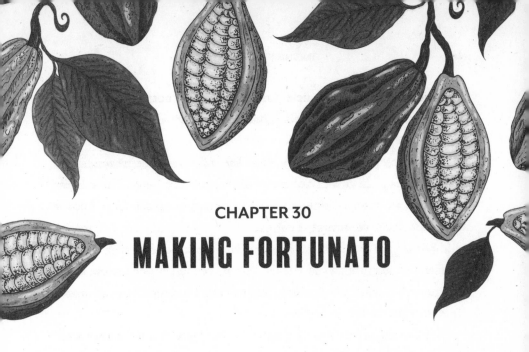

CHAPTER 30
MAKING FORTUNATO

Max Felchlin AG has a beautiful, modern factory in the quaint mountain town of Schwyz in the Swiss Alps. From the windows of Felchlin's factory you see rolling green hills and valleys with well-cared-for dairy cows grazing, golden bells on their necks, against a backdrop of snow-covered peaks. Small country houses are sprinkled throughout the valleys, sitting at the foothills of the mountains.

Sepp Schönbächler is head of innovation at Felchlin. He had received the hundred-pound sample before Dan showed up. Sepp told Dan that he hadn't seen a new origin of cacao this good in more than six years. Sepp assured Dan that the cacao was of the highest possible quality.

Not only were they impressed with the inherent flavor profile of the cacao, but they couldn't believe the outstanding postharvest processing. The Swiss are sticklers for precision in processing, and Brian had earned the utmost respect from Sepp and his team.

Dan never could have guessed how much care and attention goes into making a high-quality chocolate.

The first step was a tasting of the cacao by a panel of seven people, a process specific to Felchlin. The tasting panel was made up of longtime chocolate professionals with finely honed palates. According to the cacao's aromas and flavors, determined primarily by genetics and postharvest processing, a protocol for chocolate making was put together.

What percent of cacao would they use? What would the recipe be? Would vanilla be included? What would the roast profile look like? How long should the chocolate be conched? Everything was decided with the conscientious and scientific goal of making the chocolate as delicious as it could possibly be.

Sepp felt certain that our chocolate must be made using the old 1879 longitudinal conches. Not many origins were permitted to use those conches. There were only three machines available for use, and they weren't efficient. But for the very special origins, the old conches created unrivaled flavor.

Conching comes at the end of the chocolate-making process, after the cacao has been roasted, winnowed, ground, mixed with sugar, and refined through milling. It is the last step before chocolate is molded and cooled.

The old conches take sixty hours or more to do what modern conches do in five to fifteen hours. This allows the chocolate makers to taste throughout and decide if a particular cacao needs more or less of some ingredient. They learn whether roasting profiles need to be adjusted. They can slow down the speed of the wheel and adjust the heat. The process is artisanal. It isn't a set-it-and-forget-it process; on the old conches, the chocolate must be monitored.

While in Switzerland, Franz introduced my dad to Roger Von Rotz, owner of a chain of Swiss bakeries. Roger was well known throughout Europe for his successful business ventures, outstanding baked goods and confections, and unrelenting dedication to the highest quality ingredients.

Roger was already using Felchlin chocolate and was a longtime friend of Franz's. He visited Felchlin during Dan's trip, and was on the tasting panel that formulated our dark chocolate recipe. He was so intrigued by the story and impressed by the cacao and the chocolate it produced that he agreed to become our very first chocolate customer.

Roger Von Rotz is our exclusive customer in Switzerland to this day. If you go to Switzerland, you must visit one of his six Konditorei von Rotz locations and taste his creations made with Fortunato No. 4 chocolate, specifically his wide selection of truffles and cakes. Several years later, Roger Von Rotz also helped us develop our first milk chocolate.

On this trip, several important decisions were made. It was decided that we would immediately ship our cacao from Miami to Switzerland. Sending cacao to Switzerland requires a trip through the port of Rotterdam in the Netherlands. From the port, shipments are loaded onto a river barge. The cargo is taken off the barge at a landing and loaded onto a truck that heads due south into the Alps.

We had no experience managing logistics in Europe. Then again, we didn't have any experience with anything we were doing, so this got put on the long list of things we'd figure out as we went along.

Based on Sepp and Franz's recommendations, the president of Felchlin agreed to make our chocolate on a contract basis. This was the first time that Felchlin had ever agreed to do this for a North American company.

We'd leave some of the chocolate in a warehouse in Switzerland for Roger Von Rotz to use. We would also leave an allotment there for new customers we planned to sign up throughout Europe. Franz promised to introduce us to many more of his colleagues, and he lived up to that promise in a big way.

The rest of the chocolate would come to the United States, where we would try to sell it to restaurants and chocolatiers. Paul and Crystal at Chef Rubber generously agreed to let us use their warehouse for storage and offered to do fulfillment when we made sales. Franz, Paul, and Crystal were so generous with us.

Perhaps the most interesting, and most delicious, decision was to produce a simple, 68 percent dark chocolate as our first offering. There was a hot debate about this among the team at Felchlin, Dan, Franz, and Paul.

One side thought that the trend was toward darker and darker chocolates and that 68 percent wouldn't be dark enough. The market was becoming more interested in the health benefits of chocolate, and the benefits were more pronounced in darker chocolates.

The other side took the position that despite what people said they wanted, in every blind taste test conducted, 68 percent dark chocolate always came back as the favorite. So, the question was whether we wanted to go healthy or delicious. It was a good question, and it has shaped many of our business decisions over the years.

Our position was that my brother hadn't moved out to the jungle and built a world-class processing facility to make a health food. Cacao has equal health benefits whether you do the postharvest processing well or poorly. All of Brian's efforts were geared toward making a great-tasting chocolate, and we made the decision to hang our hat on deliciousness.

We ended up with an austere and elegant, three-ingredient dark chocolate made from pure Nacional cacao with deodorized cocoa butter for texture and cane sugar. We asked why Felchlin wanted to add cocoa butter, and they told us it would make the chocolate easier for dessert professionals to work with. We didn't know enough to argue, so we accepted their expertise. To this day, we make our 68 percent dark chocolate using the exact same recipe.

With our first customer lined up and our first product in production, Dan came home very happy and satisfied. We knew how we'd generate cash to buy more cacao. The outlines of the business were taking shape. Buy and process cacao. Send it from Peru to Switzerland. Make chocolate. Sell the chocolate in Europe, Asia, and the United States. Get good at that and keep doing it forevermore. The family business that Dan was hoping for appeared on the horizon.

A refurbished 1879 conche at Felchlin in the process of making Fortunato No. 4, 68 percent dark chocolate.

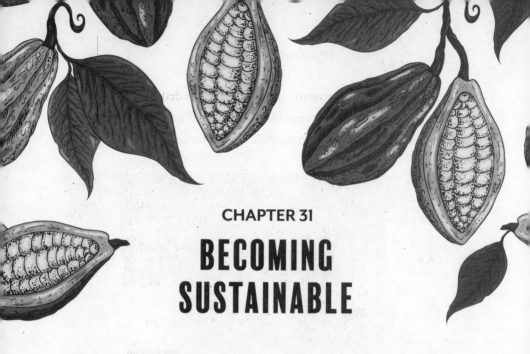

CHAPTER 31

BECOMING SUSTAINABLE

At the end of that first year's harvest, Brian worked with his team to repair worn-out equipment and change the facility's layout based on new knowledge. He spent a lot of time hobnobbing with cacao farmers out on their farms. For the company to grow, we'd need a lot more farmers in the project.

The more time Brian spent with the farmers, the more he was reminded of the debilitating poverty out in campo. The principal underlying causes were geographical remoteness and vulnerability to commodity market price swings.

One year the price of rice, coffee, beef, or cacao was up, and the farmers seemed temporarily flush. The next year, prices dropped through the floor, and folks couldn't afford to send their kids to school or pay for a doctor's visit.

He saw how certain villages were behind rivers with shoddy bridges. When the rain came, the rivers rushed over the bridges, trapping folks in their villages for weeks or months at a time. They needed enough money to buy supplies to survive those times of entrapment. If commodity prices had broken them, folks could die out on their farms, starved for basic necessities.

A typical farmhouse dining room in the district of Huarango.

Many farm women were stricken with lung sickness from cooking in tiny kitchens over cinderblock stoves, filled with burning wood. The women had to stand there breathing in wood smoke day in and day out, preparing meals, until one day they started coughing up blood.

Brian saw children with fingers cut off from working with machetes. He saw farmers with legs amputated because of infections that, in the United States, were cured as a matter of course.

He saw old men and women, backs slumped over as they bent down to pull up rice shoots, their hands and feet muddy, skin charred by the sun. These grandmas and grandpas should have been taking care of their grandchildren and dispensing hard-earned advice to the family, not using their worn-out, frail bodies to plant and harvest rice just to make ends meet.

Those huge, bright red cacao pods, the industrial hybrids, were becoming more and more common. Brian heard how, after a few years, all the other plants around the hybrids started to shrivel up and die. The soil was used up and stripped in the production of unnatural quantities of oversized pods. Eventually, synthetic fertilizers would have to be brought in to revitalize the soil. None of the farmers liked this, but they had no other choice. When market prices went down and they needed quick money, increased volume gave them a short-term gain.

Brian kept thinking about how cacao farmers are the same as everyone else. They love their families and want to fall in love, have adventures, find meaning and purpose, and help the next generation be better than their own. They are proud of their children when they act right, disappointed when they misbehave. They want to be healthy, attractive, and financially secure. They have ambitions and hopes and dreams.

Some farmers are sober, hard workers who take great pride in their farms. Others are lazy or drunk, and their farms look like nobody gives a damn.

Other than the unique and frequently harsh environment, a cacao-farming village is like any other place, and cacao farmers are just like other people.

The upshot of his awareness was that Brian was committed to doing everything in his power to help his new friends and neighbors. He vowed to run the math and pay these folks the absolute maximum our company could afford. My dad and I fought him at times, based on what we knew to be typical business profit margins, but Brian was steadfast. He had seen and heard too much.

For our business to be a long-term success, we needed a sustainable way to convince farmers to replant pure Nacional cacao. If the trend toward pulling up the native cacao variety in favor of industrial hybrids were to continue, our progress would cease just two or three years downstream.

Noé Vasquez came up with a brilliant solution. Although our funding was limited—we were still scraping by with funds borrowed from friends and family—Noé and Brian started a clone nursery. It isn't easy to think long term when you're running out of money, but Brian and Noé summoned the grit to do just that.

Noé believed it would be a tremendous boon for the community to clone the tree on Fortunato's farm that tested as the purest expression on record of pure Nacional. Brian agreed, and Don Fortunato agreed to go along with the project.

There are two ways to grow a new cacao tree in a nursery. You can plant a cacao seed, or you can make a clone. If you plant a cacao seed, it will grow up out of the soil fully formed and start producing usable fruit in two to seven years. In the case of pure Nacional cacao in the district of Huarango, the average time is two to three years before a tree produces usable fruit. Industrial hybrids in Africa can take seven years. It depends on the quality of the soil and how well the fruit is adapted to the environment.

When you plant a seed, the new tree will be a child of the tree the seed came from and the tree responsible for pollination. It will be a unique offspring of two individual trees.

If you clone a cacao tree, you take a branch off the tree you want to clone, and you graft the branch onto a root stock. In the case of this new clone nursery, Noé found two benefits that led him to favor cloning.

The most obvious reason was that we would get identical twins of the purest pure Nacional cacao tree ever tested. Every single clone would be an exact genetic match with the characteristics that Noé found so bewitching in the original mother tree.

Another big benefit is that a clone would allow us to choose good root stock. Trees are very peculiar when it comes to grafting. It is bizarre to think about, but when you graft a clone branch onto a root stock, the genetics above and below the graft remain distinct forever. The roots can have one set of genetics, and the tree above the graft will have a different set.

Noé saw this as a tremendous opportunity. In the past, he had bred trees to have excellent root stocks. He already had a collection of these trees, and he could grow more. These root stocks were very efficient at absorbing water and nutrients from the ground to nourish the fruit on the trees.

By pairing high-quality root stocks with the genetic offspring of the Fortunato mother tree, we would have the best of all worlds. It would be highly productive like an industrial hybrid because of the roots. It would be fine flavored and genetically pure because of the clone above the graft. Because the tree would be well adapted to the environment, essentially as perfectly adapted as any cacao tree could be, it would be symbiotic with the jungle, not competitive. It would be naturally disease resistant. It was a thing of genius.

If cacao farmers wanted to come into our project, all they had to do was go to Noé's farm and take away mother tree clones to plant on their farm. We subsidized the nursery and gave the clones away for free. The program wouldn't lead to any production increases for two to three years, but that was fine by us. We weren't going anywhere.

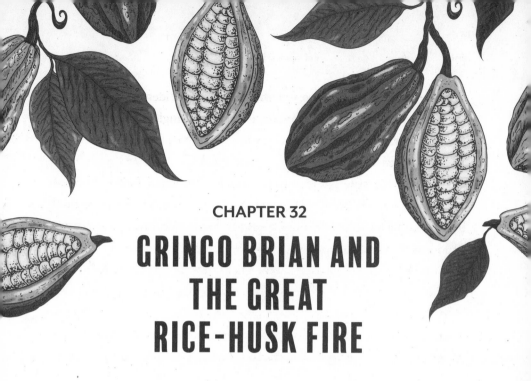

CHAPTER 32

GRINGO BRIAN AND THE GREAT RICE-HUSK FIRE

A couple of weeks after returning from Switzerland, my dad asked if I was ready to come to work for the company. Franz had helped us sign up a couple more customers in Europe, and we had chocolate coming to the United States he would need help selling.

I asked him how much the company would pay me, and he said $1,500 a month. I asked if there would be a commission structure on top of that. He said that you don't take commissions in a family business. I'd be paid more when the company made more. I told him that I couldn't live on that amount. He told me that he had lined up something else for me.

Dudley A'neals was my dad's CFO at the Horton Grand Hotel and now had his own practice doing complex tax work and accounting. Dudley was also one of the friends who had loaned money to the chocolate business to buy cacao. He needed some help and had a part-time accounting job for me if I wanted it. Between those two jobs and Nery's income, my dad figured I'd be able to get by while we grew the company.

We'd been working in Peru since 2003. I was supposed to join the business in 2006 after I graduated from college, but there was no business left. Now it was late 2010, and I was finally going to be on the payroll. I'd be receiving a small check, but at least, it was something. I quit my job and joined the company.

Through Paul Edward, we'd gotten commitments from a couple of US companies to buy chocolate, the biggest of which was Moonstruck Chocolate out of Portland, Oregon. Their chocolatier, Julian Rose, was a great friend of Paul's and Julian was very enthusiastic about our chocolate.

We'd also managed to network our way into a launch party and press conference at the Institute for Culinary Education (ICE) in New York City in January 2011.

Due to how quickly the launch party and press conference had come together, Felchlin had to send our first shipments of chocolate to the United States on two different boats. Both ended up in Chef Rubber's warehouse in Las Vegas. The first shipment was a small batch sold to Moonstruck before the launch party so that we'd have product to sell along with our coming out. The second shipment came a month later.

Meanwhile back in Puerto Ciruelo, Brian was living through a nightmare.

He and his family had come to the States for a brief visit in late autumn of 2010. It was the first time Cecilia had visited Brian's hometown of San Diego, and the first time baby Amara had traveled. Brian was excited to spend time with his family and show Ceci his world back home.

While on the trip, Brian got a call from Melko. Back then, there was no easy way to make a clear, high-quality, international call from out in campo. The reception was very spotty, and Brian couldn't clearly understand what was being said. He thought he heard the word *fuego*, "fire," but he didn't catch the context or nature of the fire. Brian told Melko that he couldn't hear too well and that he'd handle the problem when he was back in campo.

Back in Cajamarca after a relaxing and family-strengthening trip to the United States, Brian kissed his wife and daughter goodbye and made the seventeen-hour bus ride back to Jaén. He drove two hours to the Chinchipe River and crossed in a *lancha*. Thankfully, the river was low that day.

Brian recalled something about a fire, but his overriding emotion was happiness to be back at work. He was excited to see his team. He was ready to start planning for the coming harvest season. He knew some of the equipment still needed to be repaired, and he wanted to lay down a fresh layer of concrete in the fermentation room. Several new fermentation boxes had been commissioned by the carpenter.

Also, Brian had kept his promise by completing a harvest and paying top prices for the last crop. Many more farmers were ready to participate in the 2011 harvest. Several successful and respected cacao farmers had participated in our first harvest, namely Don Fortunato, Don Regulo Vargas, and a successful farmer named Don Becho. They'd been spreading the word and recruiting on our behalf.

Brian had spoken with Dan at length during his trip to San Diego. He had been updated on the Switzerland trip, heard about the European clients, learned that we had some cash flow, and knew that more chocolate to sell would arrive in the States soon. Dan told Brian about the launch party and that the *New York Times* would have a food reporter there.

Brian was pleased and proud that their cacao had received such stellar reviews. There was a lot to feel good about.

Brian's very first step into the processing facility extinguished all positive feelings. There was gray ash all over everything. It was piled inches thick on his dryer beds. It was six inches deep inside the fermenter boxes. Melko was there with a T-shirt tied around his face.

Melko waved at Brian to follow him out of the facility and onto the street. After they'd walked a few blocks, Melko took the shirt off his face and told Brian that the ash was very toxic when inhaled. Breathing it in could be fatal.

Melko explained that the rice-husk mountain had caught fire on the inside. It was smoldering from the inside out, and the wind was blowing ash into our facility. The team had tried cleaning, but as soon as they finished cleaning one section and moved onto the next, the section they had just cleaned was already covered again. It was hopeless.

Brian took off his T-shirt and covered his face with it. He started walking shirtless back toward the facility to take a look. He motioned for Melko to follow.

On the way to the facility, several local women stopped Brian in the street and asked if they could start collecting the ash in buckets to take home. Brian asked why. They told him that the ash was excellent for heavy scrubbing, such as cleaning stained pots, when mixed with water into a paste. Using this ash would save them money on buying detergent. Brian agreed, and the group of women followed along. The ash collection continued for another year until the rice-husk mountain burned itself out. At least, the families in town were able to save money on scouring powder.

Melko and Brian toured every inch of the facility, and there was no part that wasn't affected by the fire. Brian racked his brain for ideas, and something occurred to him. He remembered hearing that at one time the Central Valley of California, a huge agricultural area, grew a lot of rice. Could there be any old-timers there who knew how to put out a rice-husk fire?

The huge rice-husk mountain that caught fire behind our facility.

It was a long shot, but failure to put out this fire meant building a new processing facility from scratch. The new harvest was around the corner, and with no facility, our credibility would be shot down right when it was on the upswing. Brian would be forced to stay in campo indefinitely, working day and night, for months.

Brian made a snap decision and immediately headed back to Cajamarca where there was better internet and phone access and he could more easily makes calls to California. In campo, it was nearly impossible to call internationally.

In Cajamarca, he surfed the internet for contact information on fire stations in the Central Valley. He cold-called several, paying exorbitant long-distance charges. He laid out the conundrum, and all said they couldn't help, until Brian reached a fire chief from the city of Modesto.

The chief couldn't give any guidance himself, but he gave Brian the name and number of a previous chief who had retired a decade earlier.

Brian called the retired chief, and the fellow picked up. Brian quickly explained himself and convinced the old-timer to give a few moments of his time.

The retired fire chief explained that the only way to put out a rice-husk fire was to take sections off the top, one layer at a time, flatten them out on the ground, and extinguish each section separately. If the center of the mountain was smoldering, you'd never be able to put out the fire without taking the whole dang mountain apart. Then the fire chief asked how big the mountain was.

When Brian told him the mountain was 60 feet tall, 100 feet wide, and 150 feet long, the chief went silent. After several moments, Brian heard a low chuckle coming out of the phone. Little by little, the chuckle turned into a full belly laugh. The chief laughed so hard that he lost his breath and started coughing. Brian realized that it was a lost cause.

Brian kissed Ceci and Amara goodbye. He told them that he didn't really know when he'd be back, and he set off on the long bus ride to campo.

Back in campo, Brian leased a different abandoned rice mill four blocks up the street. He didn't have any problems or face any objections leasing the new mill, because he had already proven his seriousness and had won the respect of the community.

Brian worked day and night for two months. He spent a total of six days at home during that two-month period. The team worked 15–16-hour days out in the humid jungle heat. They didn't stop for rain. They didn't take the traditional two-hour siesta at lunch. They worked weekends. They worked straight through, driven on by their leader, "Gringo Brian."

Gringo Brian was the name the townspeople had given Brian, in accordance with the Peruvian cultural custom of giving people nicknames based on appearance.

Our second cacao processing facility in the district of
Huarango, also built in an abandoned rice mill.

As Brian didn't go home very much during this period, he started making a lot more phone calls to check in. In Puerto Ciruelo, the houses didn't have phones. There was only one phone cable coming into town, and it was split into five lines in the shop of a very colorful character. Those five lines were run into four booths for making outgoing calls; one line ran into a phone that the shop owner used for answering incoming calls.

When people called in, the owner of the shop announced the call on a loudspeaker that the whole town could hear. He'd get on his microphone and announce over the loudspeaker, "Jose, you have a call. Jose, you have a call." And then Jose would come, get the information, and call the person back in one of the booths.

Sometimes the owner of the shop would add a little commentary or make a little joke with the announcement. "Jose, you have a call. Jose, it's a woman but not your wife." As a result of this setup, everybody knew each other's business all the time, as is common in very small towns.

When Cecilia called for Brian, the shop owner always announced, "Gringo Brian, you have a call! Gringo Brian, you have a call!" The name stuck, and nobody called him anything else.

The farmers who had sold us cacao during our first harvest watched the progress of the new facility, worried that Gringo Brian couldn't finish on time. They respected his effort greatly and rooted him on. However, if the facility wasn't done in time for the next harvest, they'd have no choice but to make alternate arrangements.

Nobody in town believed that Gringo Brian would finish before the harvest. But Brian, through sheer will, pulled off the impossible. Just a few days before the harvest was to begin, the facility was done. Many more farmers were ready to throw in their lot with us. Nothing succeeds like success.

CHAPTER 33

IT'S THE GOOD STUFF

After the marathon of working in the heat, Brian's body started to give out, and he fell into a very deep funk. He went home to rest before the harvest, and when the time came to say goodbye to his family again, he didn't want to go. He called me and Dan to tell us he was thinking about quitting. His body was wrecked, and he was tired of saying goodbye to his family.

Dan told Brian to do his best and take whatever time he needed to rest, and we'd try to think of a solution. Like a true hero, Brian did not quit. He dragged his tired, dejected butt over to the bus station on schedule and went out to start the harvest as he'd promised the cacao farmers he would do.

In New York, our launch was mostly successful. The *New York Times* gave our chocolate a wonderful review that generated a lot of inbound leads.

The prospects were all fired up—until they heard the price. That took some wind out of their sails, but many still placed small initial orders.

Paul and Franz had convinced us to pursue an ultraluxury-brand concept that included pricing our chocolate 40 percent higher than the next highest-priced chocolate on the market. Our price was not only much higher than the base chocolates commonly used by chefs and chocolatiers, it was 40 percent higher than the most expensive chocolate they'd ever heard of.

The consequence of this strategy played itself out with Moonstruck after our launch. Based on the ultraluxury price we charged Moonstruck, they put their Fortunato No. 4 chocolate product online at a price six times higher than a comparably-sized bar at the grocery store.

A lot of people came online and purchased on the strength of the *New York Times* article, but there weren't many reorders. As a result, Moonstruck didn't place a very big reorder from us. Our budget counted on their reorders. That, plus the unplanned buildout of a new processing facility, put us in a dire financial position.

A week after the launch, our second shipment of chocolate arrived from Felchlin. My dad and I took a road trip to Las Vegas to see it unloaded. I remember watching Crystal drive the forklift, unloading pallet after pallet. God, did it look like a lot of chocolate. About ten tons. I looked at all that chocolate and wondered how we could possibly sell it all.

After the chocolate was unloaded, Paul called us into a meeting room, and he grabbed a box of the chocolate on the way in. He cut the box open with a knife and pulled out a block. The chocolate comes from Switzerland in big 1.1-pound blocks. Paul asked one of his workers to bring a cutting board and a chopping knife. Paul started chopping the chocolate into chunks for us all to try.

I was in a bad frame of mind, wondering what we'd gotten ourselves into. Brian was suffering. We hadn't sold much chocolate from the launch.

We'd received a lot of orders, but they were small. Moonstruck wasn't going to reup.

Thankfully, our European customers were increasing their orders. The market for high-priced chocolate was different there. The harvest was starting, and we'd have to pay Felchlin soon. Our cash position was untenable. There was no question we'd have to go hat in hand to our friends and family again.

Then I put a chunk of our 68 percent dark chocolate into my mouth. Stone fruits. Cotton candy. Roses. I looked over at my dad, and his eyes were closed. I looked at Paul. He smiled at me and said, "That's the good stuff, huh?"

Yeah, it was the good stuff. We'd figure it out. Whatever we had to do, we'd do.

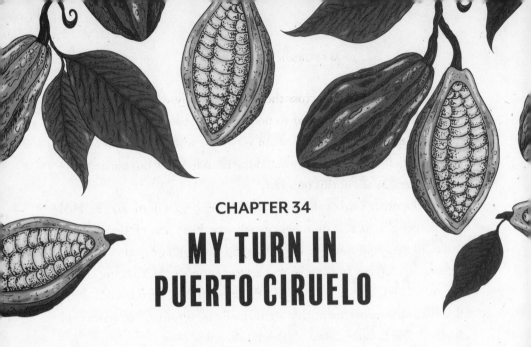

CHAPTER 34

MY TURN IN PUERTO CIRUELO

My dad and I were busting our tails trying to sell chocolate, figure out how to fix our pricing, and manage our terrible cash situation when we got a code-red call from Brian. He was working too hard. His body was giving out. His family life was falling apart. He needed help. Brian asked if I could come down to Peru.

Dad offered to take over selling. Dudley agreed to give me a leave of absence from my part-time job. He was, after all, one of the company's creditors. If my going to Peru would help us pay back his sizeable loan, he was on board.

I spoke to Nery, and she spoke to her boss at UnionBank where she worked as a teller. They gave her a leave of absence as well. It was all set. Nery and I would go live in Puerto Ciruelo for as long as Brian needed. I'd run the operation in his absence. Of course, I had no experience whatsoever buying and processing cacao or with anything else I would be doing.

As we floated on a barge across the Chinchipe, my will hardened inside of me. My strongest desire was to not let my big brother down, and that would mean proving myself through very hard work. I planned to show right away that I wasn't soft. I wanted the team to know our entire family was dead serious about this business.

On the other side of the river, the staring began immediately. Here was another gringo, this time a big gangly one. Nery and I followed Brian with our luggage in tow. We were sweating through our clothes from the exertion of carrying backpacks and suitcases under the roasting sun. It had just rained, and as we turned off the main paved road down a dirt alley toward the apartment that Brian had rented for us, our shoes sank into mud that became caked all around the soles.

Despite my best attempt to stay positive, I was disappointed with the place Brian had rented for us. It was in terrible shape, but it was the only house for rent in the entire town. Brian said he'd done his best to clean it up, but it hadn't been lived in for a while.

Poor Nery. She did her best to pretty up the place, but it simply wasn't salvageable. She lit candles and used potpourri, but those attempts were throwing pebbles into the ocean.

The house was a small, stand-alone concrete unit with a sealed, brown concrete floor and concrete walls painted red. There was a half wall in the middle separating the single room into two parts. One part could be the kitchen, the other the sleeping area. It was our choice which was which.

We had a camp stove hooked up to a propane tank. There was no sink, just a spigot sticking out of the wall outside the door. We'd have to fill up a bucket from the spigot and wash dishes outside. Brian brought us a folding plastic table. We put a towel over the table for our washed dishes. We used the plastic table as a cooking counter and place to eat as well.

Brian bought us a hay mattress that he and some of the guys from the crew had put underneath a mosquito net. It was too hot for bedding so there were no blankets, just a single sheet to sleep on.

The bathroom was in a separate structure across the yard and was comprised of a sink right next to a toilet, and a shower in front of it. Turning on the shower completely drenched everything. There was a drain on the floor so the water would flow out. You then had to wipe down the sink and toilet so as not to leave them sopping wet.

In the mornings, we had to shoo a frog infestation out of the bathroom. The sink had a leak and frogs came at night to sit underneath the dripping water. It terrified me that they were so small and could jump so high. They scared Nery even more. It was my job to go in there every morning with a broom and run them out. I said a quiet prayer every time, asking God to please make them jump away rather than toward me.

As rough as it all was, we would have toughed it out, but there was one insurmountable obstacle. On the same property, there was another small unit rented by a professor. Professors in places like Puerto Ciruelo come and go. The national government sends them to remote areas on temporary contracts. This fellow taught at the local elementary school.

He was a nice man, but had a habit Nery couldn't live with. After showering, he liked to sit in the yard, nude except for his towel. He was a heavyset, unusually hairy man. The yard was right outside our little unit. I left the house early to open the facility. School started a couple hours later. Nery could see the professor from our house, through the mosquito mesh that covered our windows. She couldn't live with that view every morning and couldn't shower with him there.

After a week, we started looking for a new place. I asked the guys in the facility if they knew of anything, and they all said no.

Between where we were staying and the facility was a house that was all boarded up with a sign over the doorway saying *Huesero*. "Hueso" means bone, and a huesero is a bone worker of sorts. They set broken bones, do chiropractic work, and will do pretty much any other thing a person will pay for that seems therapeutic.

I asked the guys about the place, and they told me it had been abandoned for five years. Nobody wanted to live there. I asked them why not, and they said, "Ratas." ("Rats.") Oh brother.

Nery still wanted to pursue renting the abandoned house. She felt a rat infestation was better than the hairy professor. Poor guy. I asked our team if they knew who owned the house, and they told me his name and where he lived.

At night after work, Nery and I knocked on the owner's door, and he greeted us. We explained our intentions, and he implored us not to rent the place. It wasn't only the rats. He was unsure of the plumbing. He didn't know if the water was still running. And the balcony behind the house, on forty-foot stilts overlooking the river, hadn't been maintained for years. We couldn't avoid going out on the balcony because the bathroom was out there.

Nery was not dissuaded and asked to see the place. The owner shrugged his shoulders and grabbed the keys. We walked through the quiet town at night. There were no streetlights. We heard the river flowing and music coming from a bar several blocks down. The owner opened the door, and immediately, we heard rodents scattering.

We hit the lights and looked at the place. It was run down. A big, empty concrete room. In the back left corner was a sink. On the back wall there was a window overlooking the balcony and the Chinchipe River. The floor was cracked, polished concrete. The concrete walls were covered in peeling white paint.

On the right wall was a door leading out to the balcony. The door swung open and doubled as a bathroom door. When the bathroom was in use, the balcony door would be left open so people knew someone was in there. The bathroom had a toilet and a narrow gray pipe sticking out of the wall. The gray pipe was the shower.

To the left, near the entrance, was a steep, concrete stairway leading up to a sleeping room. The sleeping room had a window with a mosquito mesh instead of glass, overlooking the street.

We walked over to the sink and turned on the faucet. A remnant of the day's water came out. We turned on the shower faucet, and water dripped out, drop by drop. The water seemed to run. The lights turned on. We'd have the place for ourselves. That was enough for Nery. I very deeply did not want to live here, but Nery insisted, and I relented.

The owner said we had to rent the place as it was. He wouldn't do any repairs, and we had to assume all the risk if anything happened to us, for example if the balcony fell in the river, or we were bitten by a rat in the night. We agreed and asked how much the rent would be. It came out to twenty dollars a month.

The very next day at lunchtime, we walked our meager belongings down the six-block main strip under the watchful eyes of the entire neighborhood. Now the big gringo and his wife were moving into the huesero's old place. Things were becoming more exciting all the time.

While I was at work, Nery went to the hardware store and bought paint. She mopped the floor during the day, and we painted the walls at night. When we were too tired to work anymore, we went upstairs to lie inside a mosquito net, on a hay mattress, with no blankets or sheets on top of us. It was too hot.

We closed the door and latched it so no rats could sneak in. And just when we might have drifted off to sleep, we heard them. So many of them. Squeaking and lurking around, searching for food, doing whatever rats do at night.

The next night after work, we went back to the hardware store to buy plastic bins to store our food. The store owner asked us why we wanted bins, and we told him about the rats. He asked if we wanted to buy rat poison, and I told him we sure did. I asked how to administer it, and he told me to put it in ripe tomatoes. I asked if he knew where I could find ripe tomatoes and he said he had some. His house was back behind the shop. He brought the tomatoes, we thanked him heartily, and went back to the house.

I put the rat poison in the tomatoes and left them all over the floor. We went to bed and again we heard the rats congregating and scavenging. The next morning, I came down the steep concrete steps and found a rat corpse on the floor. I'd never seen a rat that big. It was the size of a small cat. I swept the rat into a dustpan, carried it out to the balcony, flung it into the Chinchipe River, and got ready for work.

I told the guys at work about the rat, and they assured me that our rat problem would now improve. They told me that rats are smart and know how to avoid death. Case in point: of all the rats we heard, only one died even though we put tomatoes out all over the floor.

As we fell into our daily routine, we actually came to enjoy the new house. Bathing out on the balcony was something I savored. After a long, hard day in the processing facility, I came home and bathed at night. It was still hot out, and I had gotten used to using a bucket and bowl for bathing. There was running water for only six hours a day, and every family in town filled up ten or so buckets while the water was running. We used those buckets for washing dishes and clothes, flushing the toilet, and bathing. We drank bottled water.

I loved standing out on the balcony and looking at the night jungle sky. I had a view of the river, and when it was low, families would be out on the little beach, playing in the water at night. Sometimes I'd see a group of young men drinking beer and listening to music. Or a young couple standing next to the river holding hands. The river never stopped rushing, and as I scooped water over my tired body, I watched the river disappear behind a jungle mountain.

When the river was full, water came five or ten feet up the stilts and felt like it was right underneath me. I took my time out there, enjoying the feel of the cool water on my skin, watching a scene I could never have imagined growing up.

Nery volunteered giving free Bible studies in the community. We also had visitors while we were in town. Her father came for a time. She talked a friend into coming to stay with us for a while. Her older brother and sister-in-law came for a week or two. These people kept Nery company while I was working all day and, many times, late into the evening.

As for the work itself, the afternoon of my first day in town, Brian took me over to meet the team. He gave me a tour of the facility, and I was so impressed with what he had built. It was beautifully constructed, clean, and orderly.

I still remember him looking at me intently, telling me that this was our family's cacao-processing facility. It was ours. Could I believe it? No, I really couldn't. My brother never seemed like more of a giant to me. Even when I was little looking up at him, he hadn't stood bigger or stronger than he did at that moment. He thanked me for coming and gave me a hug.

He took me back to his office and showed me how to do the admin work. I took notes, and I was sure that I could do this part of the job. I told him I was nervous about managing the team. I'd never managed anybody before. He told me not to worry. He said that I was Dan Pearson's son. Leading a group of men was in my blood. That made me feel better.

Early the next day, I showed up at the facility, and Brian called for a team meeting in the fermentation room. He told everybody that he would be leaving in two days. He said that while he was gone, I was going to be in charge and that everybody should help me out until I got the hang of things. He asked if there were any questions, and there were none.

The field team went off to get their motorcycles and gear ready. Brian motioned me and about six other guys over to a fermenter box. He pointed at one of the guys and asked him to bring me a bucket. Then he said to me in Spanish, "Start scooping." One of the guys pulled the top off a fermentation box, and I got up close to it with a clear, plastic bucket.

Heat rays emanated off the cacao, and the strongest vinegar I'd ever smelled hit me right in the face. Imagine dunking your head, with your eyes open, into a bucket of vinegar. That probably only gets you halfway there, because vapor fumes penetrate your eyes and nostrils much more thoroughly than liquid.

Scooping fermenting cacao out of a fermentation box is one of the toughest jobs in our facility. You don't just expose yourself to a single blast of heat and vinegar. You keep sticking your head in the box over and over again until every last cacao bean is removed. The cacao is scooped into a mixing cart on wheels, the team hand mixes the cacao, and then we put it back in the fermenter box.

Brian left me on this job for every single box that day. Normally, you'd rotate the person doing this. Several people would take turns. Not only is the vinegar hard to deal with, but you get physically tired from scooping. I got tired very fast, but I kept going for hours. I was drenched in sweat. My eyes were bloodshot red from vinegar fumes. It was a rough first few hours on the job.

I knew Brian was doing me a favor. He wanted the team to see that I was someone to take seriously. Anyone who could be the scooper for three or four hours without a break was formidable, worthy of respect.

After every single box was scooped and stirred, it was lunchtime. Four hours had flown by. I washed my hands and stumbled home. I must have looked like a giant gringo zombie to the people of Puerto Ciruelo. I ate with Nery and then went to sleep for an hour before going back to work.

The afternoon was lighter. We worked another four hours doing less taxing work and then we waited for the field team to return. Soon we heard the roar of engines coming down the hill. One of the guys jumped up and opened the metal gate. A fleet of motorcycles and taxis came rushing in. Everybody hopped to.

That first night I came home around 11:00 PM, bone tired. Having been a salesman and an accountant working at a desk for years, I was not in good shape. When morning came, my muscles were very sore. I dreaded getting out of bed and doing it all over again. But my pride was stronger than my pain. I limped into work, ready to do whatever was necessary.

On my third day in town, Brian said his goodbyes and left me to run the show. For the next week or so, I continued to assign myself the most challenging jobs so the team could see I wasn't a flash in the pan.

One job that everybody hated was replacing metal trays underneath fermenter boxes that protected our concrete floors from mucilage runoff. Bees gathered around the rims of those pans to gorge themselves on the sugary gel.

Every day, somebody had to crawl under the boxes and empty the full pans. It was a dead certainty that you would be stung many times doing this job. I'd been afraid of bees my whole life, but again, my pride was stronger than my fear. Every day for a week, I replaced trays under fermenter boxes and got the bejesus stung out of me. I was stung again doing cacao stirs. That first week, I was stung by bees ten times a day on average, and it hurt badly.

Then an interesting thing happened. The guys on the team started offering to do the more challenging jobs. They didn't strip me entirely of my turns, but they couldn't take seeing me suffer so much. I learned one of life's most valuable lessons. If you work hard and lead by example, you don't have to boss people around. They will want to help you. You earn respect most quickly through effort and behavior, not words.

Me and the team, out in front of our facility.

As time rolled on, something else became very clear to me. We were doing important work. I could see our project's potential for improving the lives of our cacao farm partners. Brian had created a system that was painstakingly dedicated to producing quality cacao. We were looking at just about every single cacao bean five times during our process and constantly removing any that weren't perfect. All that was left were perfectly shaped, perfectly processed cacao beans.

This gave me tremendous pride and confidence that, given time, we would prevail. The product was too carefully produced, from the very origin, not to gain a following.

Along those lines, I knew that when I got back, we had to lower our prices. It was vital we thrive and grow and earn market share. Too many people depended on our success. I knew exactly what I wanted to tell future customers about our chocolate, where it came from, how it was made, what it meant to the community. Now I had seen it all with my own eyes. I knew how powerful all this would be.

During my last week in town, Brian got back to his regular schedule and started taking over again. My dad, Nancy, Nancy's daughter, Katherine, and her husband, Steve, came to stay with us. My dad brought a bunch of our Felchlin-made 68 percent dark chocolate with him.

Brian arranged with Noé for us to share the chocolate with our cacao farm partners at a grower's association meeting. This would be the first time many of these farmers had ever tasted chocolate made with their cacao.

The day of the big tasting event, we got up early and took chocolate to the meeting hall. After we had everything ready, farmers started arriving, and it became clear we would have a full house. Not only were our existing cacao farm partners attending, but also it looked like every cacao farmer in the district wanted to hear what we had to say and taste chocolate made from the local cacao.

Several women hauled a big cauldron of hot chocolate to the front of the room and told me that it was ready to serve. We'd given them chocolate in the morning, and they had used it to make hot chocolate in the local style, just chocolate melted into water.

I called one of our team members, Juan, over and asked him to help me distribute the hot chocolate. I grabbed a ladle and started filling cup after cup. Juan put them on a tray and walked around, handing them out. He came back time and time again. Once the cauldron was empty, another cauldron was brought out, then another. I figure we served about a thousand hot chocolates that day.

When everyone had been served hot chocolate, it was time for the meeting to start. Noé stood up with a microphone and asked the attendees to have a seat in the plastic folding chairs set up in rows. There weren't enough seats, and many people stood against walls around the room.

Noé made some introductory remarks about how nice it was to see everybody and that this meeting should be very exciting. This was a special and proud moment for Noé. He had recruited us to come to Huarango. He had helped us get up and running. He had introduced us to many of the cacao farmers who first agreed to sell to us. Those cacao farmers were benefitting from the project, and now his compadres were going to taste fine chocolate made with the local cacao. It was a dream come true.

Next, Brian gave a talk as an introduction to the chocolate we'd be passing out. He mentioned that we'd been working on this project going on three years now. Our family had invested our entire life savings into it. Many people thought we'd give up, but we hadn't. Many people doubted we'd build a processing facility, but we had proven them wrong. Many people couldn't believe we'd pay the prices we promised to pay. They had been wrong. We'd done it two years in a row and were just getting started. And now, we'd brought back chocolate for them to try.

There was no more room for doubting, he continued. We weren't going anywhere, and we wanted more and more cacao farmers to join the project. The chocolate they'd all be tasting was now used by some of the most respected restaurants, bakeries, and chocolate shops in the world, and it came from right there in the district of Huarango. "It comes from you all," Brian said. "It is yours. Your gift to the world. You all should be very proud. The future looks bright."

It was a stirring speech. When Brian finished, we started handing out chocolate for sampling. I watched the cacao farmers. I wanted to see their reaction. These were humble people. They lived in a remote canyon on the wrong side of a wide river that had no bridge. They were tasting chocolate made from the fruit of their land by one of the preeminent chocolate makers in the world. Their faces glowed with pride.

After the tasting and the speeches, we walked around to ask the farmers what they thought of the chocolate. By far the most common remark was that the chocolate tasted pure. It tasted like it was from there. They could feel that it was their cacao. It smelled and tasted to them like the district of Huarango.

One of the best days of our lives. This is the first time that our cacao farm partners tasted world-class chocolate made with cacao from their farms.

Shortly after that, I said goodbye to the team. Nery and I headed back to the United States after three months in campo. I was fired up and ready to start selling. I was more motivated to succeed than ever before. Brian floated several trucks of cacao across the river in 2011, each with Wili as gunman. The chaos in Shumba Alta hadn't died down yet.

We lowered our prices, and I used my new, hard-won selling points. Things started to work for us. What once seemed like an endless amount of chocolate sitting in the Chef Rubber warehouse started to dwindle. We were selling through the inventory and would need more.

We had enough money coming in to support the harvest without additional borrowing. We were able to pay Felchlin and ourselves. Franz Ziegler helped us get new clients in Germany and Austria. Through word of mouth, we received inquiries from France, the Netherlands, and Japan. The dang thing was starting to work.

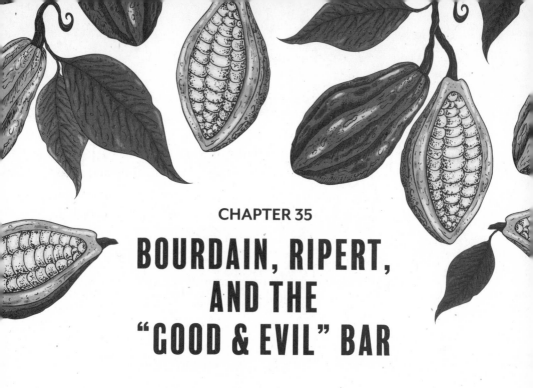

CHAPTER 35

BOURDAIN, RIPERT, AND THE "GOOD & EVIL" BAR

N ery and I moved to the Seattle area at the beginning of 2012. Nery is from the Andes Mountains, where it is cold and rainy, and she had grown tired of the hot, arid, Southern California weather.

Our time in Puerto Ciruelo made us feel confident about throwing caution to the wind. We decided we needed a new adventure. We packed a U-Haul, said goodbye to my mom and dad, and left the city where I had lived my entire life. We drove twenty hours up the coast to settle in a little town called Issaquah, seventeen miles east of Seattle.

That fall, I was invited to present at the Northwest Chocolate Festival. This was a new event put on near the Space Needle in downtown Seattle. Nowadays, the Northwest Chocolate Festival attracts tens of thousands of people from all over the region and has hundreds of booths. Back in 2012, there was one smallish room with vendor tables where attendees could sample and buy chocolate to take home.

There were a couple of stages for educational talks. In between tasting free samples, attendees could sit down and learn more about how chocolate is made and where it comes from. I put together a PowerPoint presentation with photos from my time running the facility in Puerto Ciruelo, and made a presentation about how cacao fermentation impacts the flavor of chocolate.

After my talk, several people came up and introduced themselves. Especially interesting was a young couple named Robbie and Anna, owners of Ritual Chocolate, a small-batch, craft-chocolate company. They are in Park City, Utah, now and make very wonderful chocolate. At the time, they were based out of Denver, Colorado, and working with Steve DeVries as their consultant and teacher.

Robbie and Anna told me they'd tasted chocolate made by Steve using our cacao and thought it was some of the best they'd ever tasted. They asked if we'd be interested in selling them cacao for their chocolate making. I told them that we hadn't really thought about selling raw cacao to bean-to-bar chocolate makers, so I'd have to speak with my dad and brother and get back to them.

At that time, there was a small-batch bean-to-bar chocolate movement in the United States and Europe that was picking up steam. New companies were constantly popping up. They'd buy affordable, small-scale equipment and set up shop in garages or tiny rented spaces to take a crack at making chocolate.

The ethos of this movement was to be the antithesis of large-scale, industrial manufacturing. In theory, this meant paying extreme attention to every little step in the production process. It meant producing chocolate that highlighted the unique flavor characteristics of each origin. It meant a commitment to paying high premiums over world-market prices to help support cacao farmers.

After several heated debates that sometimes devolved into shouting matches, we finally agreed to sell raw cacao to bean-to-bar chocolate companies under a different brand name, Marañón Cacao. Our arguments revolved around whether we'd cannibalize our market by competing with our own customers. In the end, we were guided by our desire to purchase increasing quantities of cacao so we could continue bringing more cacao farmers into our project.

This gave us a second market and a two-pronged approach. Some containers left Peru bound for Switzerland to be made into Fortunato No. 4 chocolate, which would be sold to high-end restaurants and chocolatiers. Some cacao came into the port of Oakland to sell to American bean-to-bar companies. As time went on, we also rented a warehouse in Amsterdam for selling raw cacao to small-batch chocolate companies in Europe and Asia.

Christopher Curtin is the owner of Éclat Chocolat. He is a talented and experienced chocolatier, operating out of West Chester, Pennsylvania. He contacted us after seeing our article in the *New York Times* and became one of our first chocolatier clients in the United States.

Chris had been working with our chocolate for over a year when he called my dad with exciting news. Chris had shared our chocolate and story with Eric Ripert, owner of Le Bernardin, a world-famous, Michelin-starred restaurant in New York City. Eric truly has too many accolades to list, but suffice it to say he is one of the most famous and respected chefs in the entire world. Eric said ours was the best chocolate he'd ever tasted.

One thing led to another, and my dad ended up in a phone meeting with Eric and Chris. The idea of us all doing a project together came up, and my dad suggested they come down to Peru to meet Brian, see our operation, and visit cacao farms. They accepted the invitation.

Several months later, Eric and Chris met Brian and Dan in the Lima airport. They flew together to Chiclayo. There, they went to open markets, visited beaches, and sampled local cuisine. Then they took the long ride from the coast, over the mountains, and down into the jungle.

The group stayed at a hotel in Jaén and made the two-hour drive out to the district of Huarango every day for a week. They motored across the Chinchipe on lanchas. They hiked on cacao farms and were treated to warm hospitality by cacao farm families. At one point during the trip, Eric put a picture online for his hundreds of thousands of social media followers. It was a picture of the humble farm meal he was eating, and the caption read that this rustic dish was more delicious than most plates you'd find in expensive restaurants.

Our visitors were beyond impressed with Brian's cacao-buying-and-processing operation. Eric and Chris rode out to farms with Brian and his team on cacao-buying trips. They saw Brian paying cash upon pickup at far above world-market prices. They saw how integrated into the community Brian had become. They saw, heard, and felt mud splattering off motorcycle wheels as the fleet drove along muddy jungle roads, moistened by fresh rain.

Dan, Brian, Eric Ripert, and Chris Curtin out in campo.

A few months after that trip, an excellent opportunity emerged. Eric Ripert was best friends with Anthony Bourdain, the famous food and travel personality. Eric wanted to release a chocolate bar in partnership with Bourdain. Anthony was admittedly not a big chocolate fan, but Eric described himself as a chocoholic, and based on Eric's enthusiasm for the chocolate and his recent visit, Anthony agreed to lend his name and media power to the project.

The bar was called the Good & Evil bar. Anthony had a reputation for being a bad boy. His raw approach to eating and travel was a big part of what endeared him to his fans. (I know, because I was one of them.) He got into the real, nitty-gritty culinary scene, not just the fancy places in big cities. He visited small towns and the countryside. He drank with locals and even ingested some of the local mind-altering substances. Anthony was the bar's "evil" image. Eric was the "good" side. The clean cut one. The technician. The pro. The expert. The one with Michelin stars.

Christopher Curtin signed on to manufacture the bar in his Éclat manufacturing facility. The bar featured our 68 percent dark chocolate and cacao nibs made with our cacao. We'd never made or sold nibs before, but it was easy to work with Felchlin to produce nibs according to Chris and Eric's desired roasting profile.

The bar ended up being sold exclusively through Williams-Sonoma, and the retail price was eighteen dollars for a two-ounce bar. There was something of an outcry over this price, and the bar didn't sell very well. The criticism of the price focused primarily on the wide spread between what cacao farmers are paid and what retailers charge for chocolate. Everybody wanted to know what part of the lofty price would make it back to the cacao farmers.

To promote the Good & Evil bar, as well as to answer critics about exploitation of cacao farmers, Anthony Bourdain decided to include the district of Huarango in an episode of his megahit TV show *Parts Unknown*. It was the Peru episode, which first aired in 2013.

The *Parts Unknown* production team worked with Brian planning the shoot. The fixer, the fellow in charge of logistics, arrived five days before

Bourdain, Ripert, and Chris Curtin. Brian took the fixer in a rented truck along the entire route from Chiclayo to Jaén, and out to Puerto Ciruelo.

Bourdain planned to spend two days shooting in the district of Huarango. On the first day, they would film a segment on Don Fortunato's farm. Under perfect conditions, it was about an hour from Puerto Ciruelo. Unfortunately, conditions looked far from perfect. It had been raining like crazy.

On day two, the plan was to visit a farm in La Mushca, a very small, remote village deep in the canyon. Getting to La Mushca was a risky two-hour odyssey traversing a half-dozen frequently overflowing creeks. When it rained hard, it was easy to get trapped out in La Mushca.

Brian took the fixer out to the villages to get a lay of the land and plan the shoots. It was raining buckets, but the fixer didn't foresee any insurmountable problems. Bourdain had traveled to remote locations all over the world, and they were used to rugged terrain.

When Bourdain and Ripert arrived in Peru, they first shot segments in Lima. When that part of the Peru episode was in the can, they made the long trek to Jaén. That first night in Jaén, my dad, Brian, Bourdain, Ripert, Chris Curtin, and the production crew ate in Brian's favorite restaurant. It was the same restaurant where Dan and Brian had eaten with Sarah Paredes their very first night in Jaén.

Bourdain broke out a nice bottle of aged whiskey, and they all drank and exchanged travel stories. Brian found Bourdain to be an extremely sweet, funny, down-to-earth, attentive, terrific person. Ripert, as always, was the epitome of a charming European gentleman. Curtin was our longtime friend and customer, and it was great having him along.

The next morning, a large caravan of trucks loaded down with production gear and personnel, drove east out of Jaén toward Bellavista. They made the left turn onto the Jaén-San Ignacio road. They stopped at the vigilante checkpoint and the vigilantes were given a peek at some unusual eye candy. They'd surely never seen so much camera gear in their lives. The caravan bounced along the terrible final ten-mile stretch that led to the Chuchuasi river crossing.

At the river crossing, the crew was confronted with challenging news. Due to recent heavy rains, the Chinchipe was too full for the barges to float across. When the river was too full and rushing too hard, the platforms could easily flip over. The barge pilots were unwilling to risk it.

The *lanchas*, canoes with outboard motors, were still working. They were being pushed far down the river before making their way back up. It looked like each one was on the verge of being swept into oblivion before finding a break in the current and working back up river to the landing on the Puerto Ciruelo side.

The caravan consisted of six good-sized, fully loaded trucks. The plan had been to drive those trucks onto the platform barges and float them across three at a time. That would mean two trips, and there were two barges, so it would have been a quick-and-easy operation. However, with the platforms out of commission, the only other option was to take all the gear out of the trucks and load it all into lanchas.

With no other choice but to get a move on, Gringo Brian started barking out orders and organizing the work. Bourdain, Ripert, Curtin, and my dad got into a lancha and crossed the raging Chinchipe. They were pushed relentlessly down river. Farther and farther, they went, their vessel unable to put up a fight against the strength of the rushing Chinchipe. The expert driver watched the water intensely for a break in the river's power and, when he saw it, swiveled the outboard motor and made a wide U-turn back up toward Puerto Ciruelo.

The gang on that first lancha went into a local cantina, drank beer, and waited. In the meantime, Brian and the production team started filling up lanchas one by one. They followed the same route that Bourdain and the group had just motored along, all the way down and then all the way back up. Transporting equipment across the river took two hours, and afterward, Brian was tired. The rain and heat had zapped his energy. Unfortunately for Brian, his endurance had only begun to be tested.

Because the trucks couldn't cross on the platform, they had to stay on the Chuchuasi side of the river, parked next to the forty-foot sheer rock wall.

On the Puerto Ciruelo side, there were no vehicles waiting to carry the equipment. Brian and the team unloaded expensive TV cameras and sophisticated audio gear out of the canoes and put it all on the street. Brian made the rounds trying to rent every single taxi in town. If they needed six trucks, they would need ten taxis.

When Brian had all the taxis lined up and paid for, and all the gear had been loaded into hatchbacks, the folks in the bar and the rest of the entourage piled into station wagon taxis. They drove out of Puerto Ciruelo and back into the canyon.

The entire filming agenda for this day was to visit Fortunato's farm and eat lunch with his family. The schedule had been delayed by the river crossing, but Brian felt they were making up time on the drive out to visit Fortunato. Things that could have gone wrong didn't go wrong. Luck seemed to be turning in their direction.

But then, in front of an uphill stretch halfway to Fortunato's farm, Brian saw a traffic jam in front of the caravan. This was bizarre because there was never any traffic on this backcountry road.

The vehicles came to a full stop, and Brian got out to investigate. He was disheartened by what he saw. The district government was installing rain drainage along the side of the road. There was a heavy tractor out there digging up dirt, and it had sunk into the mud. The driver had tried over and over to rev the motor and drive out of the rut without success. The many failed attempts at acceleration only dug the tractor in more deeply. The situation appeared intractable.

The owners of the cars stuck in the traffic jam stood around, mulling over how to proceed. The accepted conclusion was that they were all screwed. They'd have to wait for the road to dry or for the local government to tow the tractor away with another heavy machine. It would likely be several days before this would all clear up.

Brian said no. That was not how it would play out. The tractor was going to be moved right away. Everybody looked at him like he was insane and asked what he planned to do. Brian didn't know. But he sure as hell knew that Anthony Bourdain hadn't come all the way out there just to turn back around. This was a huge opportunity for our company and a chance to do a lot of good for our cacao farm partners. The answer was no; it wouldn't take several days.

Our company's employees gathered around Brian. He told them that failure wasn't an option. He wanted ideas. The team members started offering suggestions. One person said that no matter what happened, there was shovel work to be done. What if a bunch of them grabbed shovels and started digging around the tractor's tracks so there would be a path out when the time came. Brian agreed and several young men ran into the surrounding countryside to borrow shovels from local farms.

Oscar Ayala, our company's field manager, mentioned that the district of Huarango had other machines. None of us were licensed to drive them, and Oscar wasn't sure if he could find the person authorized to use them, but he could go to the administration offices to see if we could borrow one. Brian reached into his fanny pack and gave Oscar a thick stack of money. Oscar left with instructions to pay any amount necessary to get another machine over there. Money was no object. Oscar took off running uphill.

Brian told the men standing around that he would pay them for a full day's work if they could find shovels and help them dig. Several took him up on that offer and either went home to get shovels or pulled shovels out of their cars.

About fifteen men, Brian included, started digging feverishly. The rain poured down on them as they scooped and flung mud with all their might. In the middle of all this, a member of Bourdain's production team put a mic on Brian and started to film the group working.

After more than an hour, the men had excavated a good path to drag the tractor out. They took a break, and while they caught their

breath, they heard an airhorn blowing up on the hill. Oscar came running down, smiling.

He told Brian that at the government offices he'd found one of
the city's drivers doing maintenance work on a second machine. Oscar
explained the problem, and the driver said under no circumstances could
he take the tractor out without permission. Then the bargaining began.
Oscar is a shrewd negotiator, even under duress. When Oscar told Brian
how much he ended up paying, they both had a chuckle. They'd gotten
off cheap.

On top of the hill, about two hundred feet away, there was gravel on
the road, and the new tractor was able to get traction, even in the rain.
Brian and Oscar hooked a long cable to the new tractor's bumper, and
they took the other end of the cable downhill and hooked it to the bumper
of the stuck tractor.

The driver of the stuck tractor got into the cab. The driver at the top of
the hill turned on his machine and started to rev. The stuck tractor started
to slide along the groove Brian and the other men had dug. All of this was
captured on film, and the footage is probably archived on some computer
in a CNN office somewhere. We would love to find it.

After being pulled a decent way up the hill, the driver of the stuck
tractor punched his engine and took off under his own power. Everyone
cheered and shouted and jumped up and down, but the celebration was
short-lived. Now the crew had to rebuild the road and fill it with rocks so
other vehicles wouldn't get stuck. Brian and the team worked and worked,
shoveling dirt back into the rut and patting it flat before covering it with
rocks brought over from the countryside.

Two hours after the whole saga had begun, traffic started to move,
and Brian climbed back into the taxi at the front of the caravan. When he
got in the car, he looked back at the production team members in the back
seat. They were stunned by what they had just witnessed. Brian nodded
and told them, "That is how you do it. Never take no for an answer." Then

he looked over at the taxi driver and told him to get a move on. They still had a segment to film.

Bourdain, Ripert, and the fleet of taxis made it to Fortunato's farm with just enough light left to shoot. Fortunato's daughter, Johanna, and his wife, Elena, cooked a traditional farmhouse meal that greatly impressed the two world-famous chefs. Bourdain mentioned to Brian over lunch that this type of rustic meal, with fresh, simple ingredients, prepared lovingly by cooks who had been making the recipe for decades, was as good as food gets. Brian translated Bourdain's kind words for the Colala family, and they were very appreciative.

Think about it from the perspective of Don Fortunato's family. They are out in the district of Huarango. Five years earlier none of them had ever met a person from another country. Now they had a TV star and one of the most respected chefs in the world eating lunch in their humble dining room and loving the food.

At dusk, the crew drove down the repaired road and back out to Puerto Ciruelo. They loaded all the camera gear back into lanchas at the river crossing. Again, they were pushed far downriver before turning upriver on the other side, except now the sky was darkening over the jungle. On the Chuchuasi side of the Chinchipe, they loaded all the gear into the parked pickup trucks and headed back to Jaén.

Early the next day, Ripert and Bourdain went to the market to buy ingredients. They planned to cook lunch for a farm family on the second day. This trip out to campo was much smoother. The river had calmed to *mediano* overnight, and the barges were going back and forth as usual.

Hired drivers drove the pickup trucks loaded with gear onto the platforms. Everybody held their breath as they watched trucks holding $50,000 worth of high-tech camera equipment drive onto the platforms and brake just a couple feet before driving off the edge and into the river. Thankfully, the drivers were pros, and everything came off without incident.

In the tiny village of La Mushca, Don Edilberto Hernandez, known as Don Dilbe, had a grove of pure Nacional cacao on his farm with 100 percent white seeds.

Don Dilbe is the patriarch of a very big clan. He and his wife have seven children and a slew of grandkids. The Hernandez family are devout Catholics and are very upstanding people. Don Dilbe is also the long-running mayor of La Mushca.

Before hiking out to see and film the farm, which could only be reached by climbing up a long, steep hill, Bourdain and Ripert cooked lunch for the Hernandez family. It was a very sweet and humble gesture.

They prepared a wonderful meal of stewed chicken using hens and vegetables from the Hernandez farm and French-style mashed potatoes. The recipe was one part potato and two parts butter. The Hernandez family thoroughly enjoyed the meal and, at the end, asked for the secret to making such good mashed potatoes. Bourdain answered, through Brian, that the secret was the secret of most good French cuisine: butter. Everybody had a good laugh.

After lunch, the gang hiked up the big hill to see the grove of all-white cacao. Halfway up, Bourdain's lungs started letting him down, and he lamented smoking his whole life. The crew shot the segment, drove out of La Mushca, floated back across the river, and that was that.

Several months later, the show aired, and we all watched with great excitement. (You can see all of this on the Peru episode of *Parts Unknown*.) It was a fabulous episode with one glaring omission: Brian and his heroism didn't make a single appearance. That was a bit of a letdown, but the next day, our spirits were raised by the phone ringing off the hook with restaurants and chocolatiers wanting to place orders.

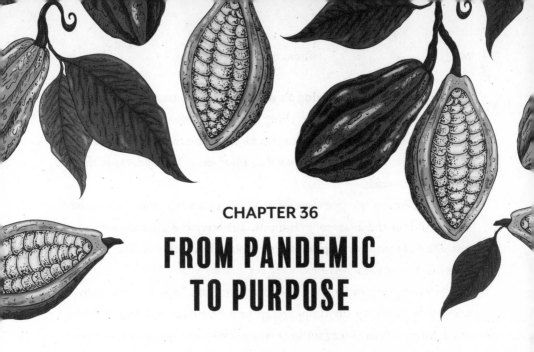

CHAPTER 36

FROM PANDEMIC
TO PURPOSE

Twice a month, or more, for ten years Brian took that long ride between Cajamarca and Puerto Ciruelo. Day in and day out, our field team drove along muddy paths to buy cacao, and our processing team processed cacao in the old rice mill. The processes kept improving and the cacao got better and better.

We floated truck after truck of cacao across the Chinchipe, and it was always just as challenging and wild. Every truck had to come out of campo and go through Jaén, over the Andes, and down the dry coast to Lima. Brian followed every truck to the port of Lima to work with the stevedores. Brian was unfailingly meticulous, as he is to this day.

By the end of 2018, we looked up, and we were doing business in more than forty countries and buying cacao from more than four hundred farm families. Our chocolate and cacao won awards at international chocolate competitions. We were featured in some of the most decorated and exclusive restaurants in the world.

During the harvest, 30–40 full-time employees worked on our buying team or at our facility. Gringo Brian had become "The Man" in the district of Huarango.

We continued to increase what we paid farmers until we reached roughly ten times fair trade premiums. Brian was the godfather to cacao farm children. Several children were named after Brian, although it was pronounced "bree-on." As time went on, our company became more and more enmeshed in the community.

We took a lot of clients out to campo to see the operation and meet cacao farmers. This was always very special and something our cacao farm partners said they enjoyed most about the project. Cacao farmers in the district of Huarango met chocolate professionals from across the globe. From a business standpoint, things were looking pretty good.

However, by the end of 2018, Brian was completely burned out on the road warrior routine. He, Ceci, Amara, and Brian's second child, Dominic, had made huge sacrifices for the business. Brian regretted missing so much of Amara's childhood. He didn't want the same thing to happen with Dominic.

Brian let us know that 2018 was his last year living in Peru. He was going to move with his family to the United States and would travel to Peru regularly to oversee operations.

He planned to leave Oscar in charge of buying and Melko in charge of processing. These two men had been with us since the beginning and ran the operation while Brian was in Cajamarca. Quality would not suffer. Those guys could and would do a great job.

This worried my dad and me, but we had to accept Brian's decision. He'd been living in Peru for fifteen years. He was the hero of our family business. He'd earned the right to do as he dang well pleased. Brian and his family moved to Issaquah, Washington, where I was living with my family. If he was coming to the United States, we wanted to be near each other.

At the start of the 2020 cacao harvest, we had five hundred cacao farm families ready to sell to us. When the COVID-19 pandemic broke out at the beginning of 2020, 95 percent of our clients got shut down. We ended up a few weeks away from having to shut down our business as well.

Peru was one of the countries hit hardest by the pandemic. In some of the little villages in the district of Huarango where we buy cacao, 10 percent of the population was killed by COVID-19. Unfortunately, the rains were fierce in 2020, making it harder than ever to get to a hospital in Jaén. Not that it would have mattered. Hospitals in Peru were so overrun that sick patients were camping out on lawns.

With shutdowns, inflation, supply chain issues, and terrible rain, our farm partners needed us to keep buying. But we found ourselves in a very weak position to be able to honor our promise of never leaving. Uncertainty swept over the world. Literally, nobody was sending us purchase orders.

Despite having no clear plan for how to recoup our money, we kept buying. It was a noble and courageous thing to do. So is stepping in front of a bullet for your family. They live and you die. They'll always remember you fondly, but you're gone and can no longer bring home a paycheck.

We looked at our bank account and watched the money dwindle. The only transactions were transfers out to Peru, no deposits. It wouldn't be long before our amazing, storied journey came to an end. We could have borrowed money from friends and family, but not with a clean conscience. It wasn't at all clear how we could pay them back.

It was a good run. A good adventure. We had the memories. After the pandemic, we'd be able to sell our stockpiled inventory of cacao. Maybe we could get the business back up and running when the world got back to normal. No one knew when that would be. The cacao farmers would have found other buyers by then. Who knows if they would start with us again? With Brian living in the United States and unable to travel due to the pandemic, our credibility would be very weak.

Just for fun, between 2018 and 2020, Nery and I had been selling individual bars of chocolate from time to time to our friends. Nery asked if she could try to sell some chocolate on Etsy. I told her to go for it. If any of our wholesale customers saw it, I'd have had some explaining to do. Thankfully, we flew under the radar.

Nery was getting five-star reviews on Etsy, and her customers were reordering. People raved about the flavor and the price. Etsy customers were getting a world-class chocolate directly from us at a wholesale price.

As our financial situation grew worse and government shutdowns became more widespread, we scrambled to pivot. It occurred to us that maybe what Nery was doing with e-commerce could be the answer. The more we thought about it, the more sense it made. We'd cut out another middleman—our wholesale clients—and sell chocolate directly to end customers. We could get an extra bit of profit while dramatically lowering the cost of world-class chocolate to chocolate lovers. Our clients marked up our chocolate 5–10 times before selling it. We could eliminate that markup.

For her side hustle, Nery was placing small orders every few months from the Chef Rubber warehouse in Las Vegas. Not much, just a few boxes.

Now we placed a very big order from Chef Rubber. We didn't have a warehouse or an office or any place to store the chocolate, nor time to get one set up. The clock was ticking, and we were running out of money. We decided to store half a ton of chocolate in my children's downstairs playroom. I hoofed it in from our porch the day UPS arrived with the shipment.

We went to Office Depot and bought shipping supplies. My dad and I worked together on an e-commerce website on Shopify. I took an online course on digital marketing and how to use paid Facebook and Instagram advertising. When our ads were running, we watched the sales numbers closely. Son of a gun. People were buying from us. We prepared those first orders right there in the playroom.

In the marketing course, I learned how to analyze advertising metrics and return on investment. I tested more and more ads and reviewed the numbers daily. One morning I noticed a particular ad was far outperforming the rest. It was a video of me explaining how our company selects out rotten cacao on cacao farms while most other chocolate companies allow rotten beans in their products.

I ratcheted up spending on that ad, and sales went up proportionally. If it kept going like that, in theory I could raise my ad spending such that we could regenerate all of our lost wholesale revenue. Each day, I spent more on ads, and it kept working. We had a successful e-commerce business bubbling. We might just be saved.

Very quickly, we realized we needed a commercial space and fulfillment staff. We rented a space in an industrial park in Issaquah. Nery had some good friends who wanted to work with us, and we hired them.

We asked Chef Rubber to send us all our chocolate. For the first time, we would be handling our own fulfillment. Chef Rubber had stored and shipped our chocolate for over a decade, and Paul and Crystal never even charged us a penny for it.

With our new space and a solid, trustworthy, hardworking team, Brian gave the thumbs-up to put my foot on the marketing gas. In a matter of months, we had over twenty thousand online customers.

Summer came, and we had to stop shipping. Without cold packing, the chocolate wouldn't survive the heat, and Brian, a serious environmentalist, felt that cold-pack materials were a no-go from an eco-standpoint. Then in the fall, with the holiday season ahead, we hit it hard. So hard we ran out of chocolate in the United States and had to call the warehouse in Switzerland and tell them to send our European inventory.

Talk about things taking a wild turn in our favor. We'd never completely sold out of chocolate before. We bought a tremendous amount of cacao during the 2020 harvest, and now we had money to start buying again in 2021. Our wonderful online customers saved us.

That brings me to the best thing about this change in direction. We got to know our customers. We were starved for that and didn't even know it.

The digital marketing course I took suggested writing a daily email newsletter sharing our story with customers. That was unknown territory for me, but so was everything else we'd ever done.

I started writing about my brother's time in the jungle, how cacao farmers lived, our postharvest process, and what it takes to make really good chocolate. I wrote about paying large premiums to our cacao farm partners while making our fine chocolate affordable, and about how our online customers saved us. I told about being a foreigner doing business in Peru, about learning Spanish, and falling in love. I opened it all up.

Folks started replying, saying how much they enjoyed learning about our journey and how much they loved our chocolate. They encouraged me to keep writing and sharing.

For the longest time, we'd been doing all this hard work, taking risks, making sacrifices in the name of a family business. It never occurred to us that we didn't even know who was eating our chocolate or how profoundly good it would feel to know them.

I sometimes tell Brian that maybe we should have been working our current model all along. He responds that maybe we weren't ready for it.

Maybe we needed a story to tell. Maybe we needed to feel the absence of interacting with our customers to truly appreciate it. Maybe so.

For me personally, our forced pivot made me feel that my dad and I had stepped out from a giant shadow that had followed our lives. Now we are doing what we were born to do. Welcoming our customers in, giving them something wonderful to eat, getting to know them. Living the legacy of my grandfather, Victor Wick.

CHAPTER 37

OUR RETAIL JOURNEY

E-commerce went well in 2020 and got off to a fast start in 2021. We had outgrown the space we'd rented. However, after being furloughed two summers in a row, our excellent and loyal fulfillment team didn't think they could stay with us through another hiatus.

Some other companies might just accept that fulfillment is a seasonal, high-turnover position. We're used to team members staying with us over the long haul. That's how we like it. The folks who run our team in Peru have been with us from the very start. Our mantra in Peru was to never leave our partners. That's what we wanted in the United States, too.

We brainstormed solutions for more fulfillment space and how to keep our team working in the summer. An agent took us on a tour of available spaces. The first place we saw was three times too big for our current needs, but standing in it, an idea hit us. Why not open a chocolate shop in this space? We could do online fulfillment in one corner and sell chocolate to the public in the rest.

There were big problems with this concept. We only had three products to sell online: our dark chocolate and two milk chocolates in the big 1.1-lb. bricks from Felchlin. Who in their right mind makes a trip to a chocolate shop with such limited selection? Also, the space was in an industrial area with no foot traffic. Last but certainly not least, retail was going through its worst downturn in history because of the pandemic.

All valid reasons to say no. But we had a great team, and none of us wanted to lose even a single player. It appeared we'd have enough space to build a kitchen and start making additional products. Perhaps our team could work on new product ideas, and we could come up with cold treats to sell in the shop during the hot weather.

As for the foot-traffic issue, I pledged to do whatever it took to get people into the shop. I'd run digital advertising. I'd walk around handing out flyers. I'd beg and plead. And the icing on the cake: we'd give away free hot chocolate all day every day to lure visitors in. Our little town of Issaquah is very supportive of locally owned businesses. We'd just have to get the word out.

In November 2021, we moved into our new, bigger space and opened the world's most austere chocolate shop. In one corner, we had a shipping station with a table and shipping supplies. In another corner, we had a bunch of chocolate sitting on wooden pallets, just as it comes from the manufacturer.

Running through the middle of this big empty room was a counter that Nery built with kitchen cabinets and butcher block from Home Depot. She painted the counter baby blue. On the counter we had jars filled up with samples of our three products along with a hot chocolate machine.

That was the whole shopping experience when we opened. Customers came into a big empty room with Peruvian music playing on a Bluetooth speaker. We offered them a free hot chocolate with whipped cream and marshmallows. It took us fifteen tries to come up with a perfect hot chocolate recipe. In the end, it was two parts dark chocolate and one part milk chocolate melted into water using a small hot chocolate machine we purchased on Amazon.

Customers could sample the three products on the counter and buy a 1.1-pound block of chocolate. Our first customers thought the whole set up was a bit weird, and I don't blame them. But it wasn't as weird as processing cacao in an old parking lot in northern Peru or sleeping in a room full of roaches. That's how it goes. You just get started and figure it out as you go along.

At the beginning of our retail journey, we caught a lucky break. We had known our fulfillment team leader, a lovely woman named Rosa Valencia, and her family for many years. We're all in the same religious congregation together. Rosa's husband, Javier, was out of work at that time and looking for something new.

Javier had been a cook for more than twenty years. He was a kitchen manager in the Amazon cafeteria back when it was still a startup, and Javier knew Jeff Bezos personally. For the last several years, he'd owned a cake business but was burned out on taking phone calls from stressed-out people wondering when their cake would be ready. He just wanted to make beautiful and delicious things, not deal with the minutiae of running a business.

From time to time, Javier put in a few hours helping Rosa with fulfillment. He knew what we were up to. When Javier heard that we were going to open a shop and only had three products, he told Rosa he wanted to help.

I was thrilled to hear that because I wanted to get out in the neighborhood to promote the shop. We needed someone to hold down the fort. Javier agreed to work in the shop and take care of customers should there be any. In the downtime, which was just about the entire day, he'd try to make some products.

We asked him what he needed to start experimenting. He requested a couple of metal tables, a couple of melters, and a small panning machine for coating nuts and other small piece items with chocolate. The small-scale equipment was pretty cheap, and we bought it all right away.

Everything showed up, and we got it installed. Then something amazing and surprising happened. Javier started creating a stream of unique and delicious products. And along with the products came customers and word of mouth. Our first retail store started to take off.

One night I came into the shop after spending several hours out and about talking to people in the neighborhood. Javier was still there, working late. Sales had gone well that day, and he had been busy with customers. He was just getting around to doing some creating. When I walked in, he handed me something that he'd just made. It was a s'more made with our 68 percent dark chocolate. When I tasted it, an entire concept came crashing down on me: we needed to become a manufacturing company.

The thing about Javier's s'more was that it straddled a line. Kids would love it. It had the delicious marshmallow and honey graham cracker. But adults would like it too because it had the world-class, elegant Fortunato No. 4 dark chocolate on the outside. It wasn't too sweet. It had interesting textural contrasts. It was easy for us to make, and the ingredients were readily available. It seemed to me a thing of perfection.

It turned out this was not a fluke. Javier has since created dozens of products that straddle that line—high-quality chocolate products that will impress foodies while still being accessible to kids and other folks looking for chocolate fun, not a heady, esoteric experience. His creations are never too sweet and always have superb texture and flavor balance.

We decided to use most of our new space for building out a commercial kitchen and production facility for Javier. We could start putting Javier's new products online and could become one of the only vertically-integrated, direct-selling, chocolate-product-manufacturing companies in the world.

Get a load of what that means.

We buy wet cacao right off the trees and ferment and dry all the cacao ourselves, same as always. The postharvest processing is still done according to Brian's specifications and is still managed by the same team that has always done it.

Oscar Ayala, one of our very first employees in Peru, still runs our buying operation. Melko, Brian's longtime roommate, still leads our postharvest processing day in and day out. Brian travels to Peru frequently to keep an eye on things.

We still move processed cacao across the Chinchipe River. In 2017, the Peruvian government built a bridge over the river, a huge blessing. The cacao still spends seventeen hours in a freight truck through the Andes and down the coast to Lima. Oscar still goes to the port of Lima to work with the stevedores.

The cacao still goes through the Panama Canal, across the Atlantic to the port of Rotterdam. The containers of cacao still go on barges and trucks to be made into Fortunato No. 4 chocolate on century-old conches by our longtime wonderful partner, Max Felchlin AG in Schwyz.

We leave an allotment of chocolate in Europe for wholesale customers, and the rest comes back across the Atlantic to the port of Houston to clear customs. Then it travels on a refrigerated truck to our commercial kitchen and manufacturing facility in Issaquah, Washington.

In the Issaquah kitchen and store, Javier leads a good-sized team that makes whatever products he dreams up for us to sell.

We own the cacao and chocolate from the time it comes off trees in Peru until the moment our customer picks it up or it shows up on their doorstep.

We refuse to sell to any big retail outlets. Although many buyers have reached out to us, we won't work through any distributors. The concept we've seized upon is to cut out every single middleman we can, give the markups back to our cacao farm partners, and pass on savings to our customers. Because of this model, very few companies can sell a product of such high quality for as fair a price as we do.

Another reason we don't sell to retailers or through distributors is that we never want to sacrifice the relationships we've forged with our customers. Call us old-fashioned, but we cherish interactions with our customers. We never want to give it up.

We know what it feels like to wholesale chocolate. It's not for us. Beyond economics, we found we have a soul purpose for not wanting someone else to distribute our products. If this limits our scale, so be it. It's limited anyhow because we still only buy one type of cacao, the formerly thought-to-be-extinct pure Nacional cacao that grows naturally in the district of Huarango. The supply only grows at 10–15 percent per year as new cacao farmers plant clones from our nursery.

We put several new products online, and they sold well. The manufacturing operation got very busy. Javier was able to handpick a team. Just like that, his ideas turned into an operation. Our new space rapidly filled up with machines and worktables and employees. It became clear that we'd need another purely retail space.

In the summer of 2022, we started looking around for a small space to test out a "purely retail" concept. Javier and his team would do the manufacturing, then we'd bring the finished products into the retail store.

We'd keep giving away free hot chocolate. It draws a crowd and creates a community atmosphere that we love, with all kinds of people from the neighborhood hanging around, catching up, sharing news, drinking hot chocolate out in front with Peruvian music in the background.

We also felt the new shop would be synergistic with our online business. We could test out new ideas on customers in the shops before offering them to the wider e-commerce audience. We need to produce a lot of inventory before putting a new product online and don't want to get stuck with products that don't sell well.

In June of 2022, we came across what looked like a perfect spot five blocks from our production facility. It was a small unit, tucked in a corner between big retailers with lots of traffic. We have REI and Safeway on one side, Target on the other. The space is only six hundred square feet with no amenities to speak of. We don't need much, just space for a counter, some shelves, and a hot chocolate machine.

Nery designed the space, and we worked as family getting it ready for launch just a few weeks after signing the lease. Those were long days. Our kids watched movies sitting on the floor in a corner while Nery and I built cabinetry and hung canvas pictures of cacao farmers and the Felchlin factory. We like sharing with our customers where chocolate starts and how it's made.

In July 2022, the second location opened. It was an immediate success. I had been researching online, learning about the margins and numbers of a good retail food business. In our first month, we did numbers that Howard Schultz described as "world class" in our little six hundred square foot shop.

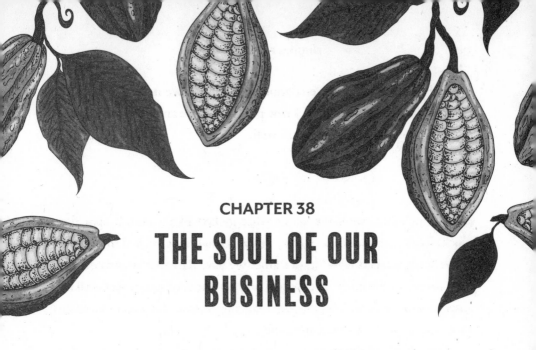

CHAPTER 38
THE SOUL OF OUR BUSINESS

On Saturday mornings, Brian and I work an owner's shift together in the new retail shop. During the week, we don't see much of each other. We each manage separate parts of the business. He runs our operation in Peru, online customer service, and our fulfillment operation. My dad manages our finances and logistics. With the help of my wonderful wife, Nery, I run the shops, oversee the production, do the sales and marketing, write the daily emails, and for the last year, I have worked on writing this book.

On Saturdays, Brian and I get to spend five hours together serving customers and reminiscing. I remember when I went down to Peru to take over for Brian and I saw our cacao-processing facility for the first time. Brian had asked me if I could believe we had our very own cacao-processing facility; I couldn't believe it.

I have the same feeling now when I work with Brian in our shop—I can't believe it. A bartender and a kid who got kicked out of college walk into a chocolate shop. It sounds like the setup for a joke, but it is real. And it is the best.

We have an amazing e-commerce business and a retail model that works very well. There are lots of options for us. We could open a bunch of company-owned stores. We could focus on expanding our manufacturing and growing the online business.

For the first time in our company's history, we don't have to allow circumstances to dictate our choices. We get to choose for ourselves what we want to do. If we do right by our cacao farm partners, make great chocolate, provide great service, make really good, fairly priced products, and spread joy, we get to decide.

I've never seen my brother so at peace. He lives in Issaquah with his son, Dominic, and his wife, Ceci. His daughter, Amara, recently moved back to Cajamarca to finish high school. She likes the United States, but her heart is in Peru. Brian has taken up snowboarding. He gets to see his son and wife just about every night. He talks to Noé and Oscar and Melko on the phone every day and goes to Peru several times per year. He works out of an office. The rambling man has settled down.

Writing this book, I've come to understand my brother, Brian, much better. From a very young age, Brian was used to moving and running and having adventures, scrambling from one thing to the next. That is how he was brought up, and he didn't know any other way.

But I believe that in the very deep, hidden recesses of his rambling heart, what Brian has always yearned for is stability. That can be in short supply for the kids of entrepreneurs.

Brian fought for his stability, and he earned it. He had to trek out to the jungle every two weeks for ten years to earn the right to live life on his terms. He had to sleep in a roach-infested building. He had to fall off his motorcycle a hundred times. He's had surgery on both of his shoulders, busted up from carrying too many hundred-pound sacks of cacao over the years.

When I see Brian in the shop on Saturday mornings, I see pride and serenity on his face. I see a man who made it out the other side. I personally can never let die what he has achieved. I won't.

As for me and my dad, I think we are finally doing what we were put on this planet to do. I believe we are all made for something. Not necessarily spiritually or in a predestined way—we all have free will and make our choices. But none of us ever really escapes the imprint of our families. I believe that in my dad's and my DNA are the building blocks of small-town food entrepreneurs. In our hearts and genes, we are pie-and-coffee men.

Life is a journey of self-discovery. My dad thought he wanted to get rich like Vic Wick for a long time. He tried his hand at raising cattle. He built a hotel. Then he realized that what he really wanted was a family business. He and Brian sold mining equipment. They tried to get a trout project going and then do an ethanol deal. In the end, the company that has endured, and that will endure for many generations to come, is the family-farm-based chocolate company with a small-town retail presence.

Like I said, my dad isn't your normal business-book hero. He is an eighty-three-year-old man with millions of dollars tied up in cacao that is sitting in bags in a warehouse in Switzerland. He owns a brand that is worth tens of millions of dollars that we're never going to sell, so he'll never get a cash payout.

But he found who he was supposed to be in the end, and because of him, I found out who I am supposed to be. If his Hindu beliefs are right, his soul has most certainly evolved this time around, and he'll be moving up.

As for me, I am a forty-year-old man. I still have a long time to go in this business. I hope that one of my three sons or one of Brian's two kids will want to take this thing over when we're done so that the family business can live on for many more generations. We've already got our kids working in the shops; they are starting young.

But here is one thing I'm not going to do, ever: I'm never going to try and be something I wasn't built to be. I am Vic Wick's grandson. I'm the son of Dan Pearson and Kit Goldman. I'm not taking off the white apron or the cacao-pod costume. Our growth as a business must be based on who we are and what we were made to do. We're cacao buyers and processors. We're a Peruvian-American family. Brian is godfather to the children of cacao farmers.

I'm not a spreadsheet man, and I don't do investor relations. I serve hot chocolate with whipped cream and marshmallows. So, if you're in Issaquah, come on by for a free hot chocolate and free samples, you hear? Feel free to stay awhile. We're there every Saturday morning. You know where to find us.

CHAPTER 39

SOME LESSONS LEARNED

I offer this final chapter to you in all humility. It feels somewhat presumptuous for a man who is likely only halfway through his life to make an attempt at dispensing wisdom. Thankfully, I have the experiences of older and wiser folks against whom to compare my observations—my dad, my brother, my mom, Don Fortunato, Noe Vasquez, and so many other wonderful people who influenced and informed our Peruvian business journey for two decades.

My dad's favorite expression is "If you never quit, you never lose." I believe this with all my heart. My father is a living, breathing example of this dictum. Despite failing over and over again, he never threw in the towel on his dream of launching a family business that could endure. Even in his darkest days, hope and optimism continued to shine through. If he was still in the game, there was still a chance. Knowing this carried us all through many hard times. A commitment to keep going, to keep trying no matter what comes our way or how impossible things seem, is truly one of the most powerful forces in the world.

Two of life's most consequential realities are that you don't choose your parents, and you don't choose where you are born. Your parents could be loving and supportive or cruel and abusive. You might be born in Bel-Air and live in a mansion, or born on a cacao farm in northern Peru and live in an adobe shack. These things are not your choice, yet they determine so much. Very few people ever fully escape the imprint of their families or the places and circumstances of growing up.

To my mind, it logically follows that we must have extreme gratitude when dealt a good hand. Likewise, we must be as charitable and empathetic as possible toward those born into greater challenges.

From long experience doing business with our wonderful cacao farm partners, who live in a remote and difficult environment, I know in my heart that very few people want or feel good about a straight handout. What feeds the human spirit is the opportunity to advance through hard work. Opportunity is the lifeblood. Providing opportunities is a huge part of our collective human mission.

My brother and I were richly blessed being children of entrepreneurs. It gave us the benefit of welcoming adventure and challenges of the unknown. That was the luck of our draw. We don't fear taking chances on something new, failing in the beginning, and figuring things out as we go. Not knowing everything in advance is part of the fun and the magic.

So, can those not born to entrepreneurial parents still walk this walk? Absolutely. There's an infinitely open market for opportunity and adventure. It takes even more grit and determination to go for it when bold risk-taking isn't part of your family's fabric as it was for me and Brian. By putting one foot in front of the other and embarking on the journey, you're almost guaranteed to get lost a few times along the way, and will probably end up digging yourself out of quicksand a time or two. You may even fall off a cliff and find yourself clinging for dear life to the side of a mountain. But when all is said and done, and you finally get where you're going, you'll know that adventures are a big part of what makes life worth living. Go on some adventures, my friends! Go on many!

As for our adventure, the only reason we were able to break into the chocolate industry with no experience and no track record is because our product was world class. If the product is deficient, the best story in the world is meaningless. You might make one sale on the strength of a story, but you won't get a reorder, and without reorders, you don't have a business.

My brother, Brian, our hundreds of cacao farm partners, our team in campo, our chocolate-making partner Max Felchlin AG, and our team in Issaquah, Washington, are dedicated to the highest quality products and top-notch customer service. Great products and great service can go a long way toward making up for lack of experience or established reputation. Focus on quality and service above all else. That allows things to fall into place.

One thing you learn from traveling and doing business abroad is that everybody everywhere is really the same. Skin color, language, and cultural differences are surface variations. With few exceptions, everybody is looking for the same things in life. They want to love and be loved. They want satisfying work that fulfills their life purpose. They want to take care of their family. They want to have fun and laugh. They want to go on adventures. They want to develop some kind of spirituality. They want to battle on the side of good when confronted with evil. They want to be happy.

Cultures tend to be different means to the same ends. When you come across something foreign that seems weird, just remember it may well be an attempt to achieve the universal goals we all, as humans, are chasing. Just in a different way. When you look at things through that lens, you can become a great observer and admirer of fellow beings from all walks of life. You'll be able to fit in and thrive anywhere.

Food production, in general, and chocolate production, in particular, is almost entirely blue-collar work. Food is only fancy and elegant at the very end of the process. Prior to the moment when that bit of elegance is finally presented to you, food work is hard physical labor, accompanied by dirt, animals, creepy-crawlies, frogs, sweat, blood, trucks, boats, machines, mountains, oceans, deserts, forklifts, bad backs, hernia belts, sore feet, sore backs, sore legs, and surgically repaired shoulders. All of that so that you can eat something delicious.

We owe it to the process to buy high-quality food and relish it. Food is one of life's greatest joys and most potent uniters. Very few things bring people together like a good meal. Eat good food and finish your plate!

We have found a way to produce high-quality food at a fair price and take better care of the farmers who grow the ingredients we love and who are extremely vulnerable to swings in world commodity prices. That way is to cut players from the supply chain. Our chocolate model can be carried out on a much larger scale and across many industries.

There are gigantic business opportunities in consolidating and vertically integrating food supply and distribution chains.

There are seven or eight players in most food supply chains who simply "hot potato" ingredients and products without adding any value. They buy and sell quickly and take a markup. Strongly funded companies who can carry inventory longer and eliminate markups can make healthy profits, manufacture better products, and take better care of farmers. The status quo is ripe for disruption.

Finally, a word about troubled youths. I was one. My brother was one. We both dealt with bad substance abuse problems in our younger years. On paper, neither one of us seemed destined for anything anyone would want to write about.

I've come to believe that traveling abroad is great medicine for a youngster going through hard times. It changes your perspective. It makes you wiser. It makes you realize how small your own personal world is. Your seemingly grave problems look a lot different in the context of what others are living through. If you know somebody who needs a new way of looking at things, consider sending them to a country where things are completely different. A plane ticket and room and board for a month doesn't have to be prohibitively expensive, but the results can be priceless and lifelong.

If you've enjoyed this book, please check out our website, www.fortunato chocolate.com. Like I said, a story doesn't mean anything if the product isn't good. Please put us to the test! Also, we'd love to see you someday in one of our retail locations in Issaquah, Washington. If you'd like to follow the continuing development of our company, I write a daily newsletter that you can subscribe to on our website. Believe me: we've got bountiful adventures coming in the decades ahead, and it is our great and heartfelt pleasure to share the ride with you—our wonderful friends, customers, and readers.

ACKNOWLEDGMENTS

This book would not have been possible without the help of the following wonderful people. My mom, Kit Goldman, for her tremendous help in editing and rewriting the book. My aunt, Michole Nicholson, for her editing assistance and encouragement. Janice Feldman for her insistence that we had a story worthy of a book. Darlene Chan, my agent, for taking a chance on somebody with no writing experience. Matt Holt for suggesting that I write the book myself instead of hiring a ghostwriter. Katie Dickman for her tremendous editorial help and encouragement. My brother, Brian, the giant. My dad, the toughest man I know. The love of my life, Nery, for inspiring me every day. Our five hundred cacao farm family partners in Peru who make our business possible. And our thousands of customers in Issaquah and across the country who continue to fund our work. Thank you all.

ABOUT THE AUTHOR

Adam Pearson is a successful entrepreneur who has been involved in growing several multimillion-dollar businesses across different industries. But his proudest accomplishment to date, besides having great kids and a wonderful marriage, is the success of his family business, Fortunato Chocolate. Along with his brother and father, Adam has been responsible for putting a rare and exquisite chocolate into the hands of tens of thousands of customers all over the world.